# YEAR 6 SATs

# SPELLING WORKBOOK

## KS2 English

### Ages 10-11

**2020-2021 Edition**

## ABOUT THIS BOOK & HOW TO USE IT

Packed with **focused practice questions** and a **wide variety of exercises**, this targeted workbook is designed to help **Year 6 students master** all the areas of **English spelling** required for the **Key Stage 2 SATs exams**. Written in line with the new testing requirements, this workbook contains:

- **25 themed units** which deal with **ALL the spelling rules covered in KS2 (Years 3-6)**
- **5 revision units** made up of **60 spelling tests**
- More than **30 different question formats**
- Over **1,800** level-appropriate **target words**, including all **200 words** contained in the government's **word lists** for Years 3, 4, 5 & 6
- **Complete Answers**
- A **Words in Focus** section listing the **target words in each themed unit**

As the Units in this book are themed, they can be **worked through in order or used for focused practice**. (Please note, though, that the words in the units become progressively harder.)

**Each Revision Unit** is made up of **12 Spelling Tests** that assess the spellings covered by the **previous five units**. We recommend that students are given as much time as they need to complete them.

**Most of the questions** in this workbook have **only one correct answer**. When there is **more than one** possible correct response, this is **indicated in the Answers**.

## Before you get started...

This book comes with FREE printable Self-Assessment Sheets & a Test Diary for students plus a Complete Spellings List.
To access them, simply visit our website @ https://bit.ly/2XYr3AG or use the QR code below:

Published by STP Books
An imprint of Swot Tots Publishing Ltd
Kemp House
152-160 City Road
London EC1V 2NX

www.swottotspublishing.com

Text, design, and layout © Swot Tots Publishing Ltd

First published 2017 by Swot Tots Publishing Ltd
This edition published 2020 by STP Books

STP Books have asserted their moral right under the Copyright, Designs and Patents Act, 1988, to be identified as the author of this work.

Typeset, cover design, and inside concept design by Swot Tots Publishing Ltd.

British Library Cataloguing-in Publication-Data. A catalogue record for this book is available from the British Library.

ISBN 978-1-912956-21-0

# CONTENTS

> **For each of the following, underline the one correct spelling from the choices given in brackets.**
>
> *Example:*  **The bird chirped (merryly  merrily  merilly  merrilly) in the summer sun.**
> The bird chirped (merryly  <u>merrily</u>  merilly  merrilly) in the summer sun.

1. "I think I'll go out (tomorrow  tommorrow  tommorow  tomorow)," said Jim.

2. 'Ali Baba and the (Fourty  Fouty  Forty  Fourtie) Thieves' is a well-loved story.

3. Shaun always (criticises  critticises  critecises  critiscises) everything.

4. The (identite  identity  identaty  identtity) of the winner is not yet known.

5. I love the (variaty  varyty  varriety  variety) of fresh fruit at the local market.

6. The parcel will (probably  probibly  probbably  probabley) arrive after Christmas.

7. Elias looked very (awkuard  awkwad  awkward  awkould) in his new suit.

8. The toilet has been (occuppied  occupied  ocuppied  occupyed) for ages!

9. Scientists are (developing  developping  develloping  develaping) a cure for this.

10. The man's face looked very (familyer  femilyer  familar  familiar).

11. Omar raised a (relavant  relivent  relevant  rellevant) point during the discussion.

12. Despite being an (amatuer  amateur  amator  amature), Lucy is a talented singer.

13. John was being (harassed  harrassed  herassed  herrassed) by a persistent salesperson.

14. There has been a (defanite  deffinite  definite  deffinnite) change in the weather.

15. We can't wait for the (twefth  twelth  twelf  twelfth) season of our favourite TV show.

16. Last (Wensday  Wendnesday  Wednesday  Wendsday), we went to the cinema.

17. I have (attached  attatched  attacthed  attacht) the document to this email.

18. The island has been struck by a (categry  categary  category  catigory) 6 hurricane.

19. I walked into the end of the bed and (brused  bruised  brewsed  briused) my thigh.

20. They had a (wunderful  wanderful  wonderfull  wonderful) time with their cousins.

---

> **25 words are listed below. However, 10 of them are spelt incorrectly. Find the 10 incorrectly spelt words and write their correct spellings in the spaces provided.**

| | | | | |
|---|---|---|---|---|
| accident | occassion | cemetery | parliment | recognise |
| dictionery | sincere | determined | explaination | signature |
| queue | embarass | programe | community | compitition |
| guarantee | vehicle | physical | corespond | eight |
| nieghbour | accompany | secretry | yacht | available |

21. _____       26. _____

22. _____       27. _____

23. _____       28. _____

24. _____       29. _____

25. _____       30. _____

---

> **In each of the following, show whether the given word is spelt correctly or incorrectly. If the word is incorrectly spelt, write the correct spelling in the space provided.**
>
> **_Examples:_**   chair      ☑      _____
>
>                saveing      ☒      _saving_

31. neccessary    ☐    _____

32. goverment    ☐    _____

33. pronounciation    ☐    _____

34. tempreture    ☐    _____

35. according    ☐    _____

36. vegtable    ☐    _____

37. individual    ☐    _____

38. restraunt    ☐    _____

39. excellent    ☐    _____

Complete the following tables, showing whether each word has been spelt correctly or incorrectly.

_Examples:_

| WORD | Correct | Incorrect |
|------|:-------:|:---------:|
| _lazy_ | ☑ | ☐ |
| _funnie_ | ☐ | ☑ |

| WORD | Correct | Incorrect |
|------|:-------:|:---------:|
| 40. dissapear | ☐ | ☐ |
| 41. strenght | ☐ | ☐ |
| 42. build | ☐ | ☐ |
| 43. medcine | ☐ | ☐ |
| 44. excercise | ☐ | ☐ |
| 45. group | ☐ | ☐ |
| 46. circle | ☐ | ☐ |
| 47. straight | ☐ | ☐ |
| 48. adress | ☐ | ☐ |
| 49. calander | ☐ | ☐ |
| 50. seperate | ☐ | ☐ |
| 51. ordinray | ☐ | ☐ |
| 52. fruit | ☐ | ☐ |
| 53. imagine | ☐ | ☐ |
| 54. paticular | ☐ | ☐ |
| 55. hieght | ☐ | ☐ |
| 56. learn | ☐ | ☐ |
| 57. recent | ☐ | ☐ |
| 58. natural | ☐ | ☐ |
| 59. favorite | ☐ | ☐ |
| 60. often | ☐ | ☐ |

| WORD | Correct | Incorrect |
|------|:-------:|:---------:|
| 61. quarter | ☐ | ☐ |
| 62. actually | ☐ | ☐ |
| 63. thorugh | ☐ | ☐ |
| 64. strange | ☐ | ☐ |
| 65. suprise | ☐ | ☐ |
| 66. popular | ☐ | ☐ |
| 67. rememember | ☐ | ☐ |
| 68. breathe | ☐ | ☐ |
| 69. consider | ☐ | ☐ |
| 70. deciede | ☐ | ☐ |
| 71. certain | ☐ | ☐ |
| 72. pehaps | ☐ | ☐ |
| 73. purpose | ☐ | ☐ |
| 74. centry | ☐ | ☐ |
| 75. intrest | ☐ | ☐ |
| 76. important | ☐ | ☐ |
| 77. therefor | ☐ | ☐ |
| 78. sentance | ☐ | ☐ |
| 79. grammer | ☐ | ☐ |
| 80. desperate | ☐ | ☐ |
| 81. earth | ☐ | ☐ |

---

**Each of the following sentences contains ONE spelling mistake. Find the misspelt word and underline it.**

*Example:* **The young boy's behavior was terrible.**

The young boy's <u>behavior</u> was terrible.

---

82. Much <u>controvesy</u> surrounds this painting; many people believe it is a forgery.

83. We were all impressed by Maria's <u>determinacion</u> to compete in the race.

84. The meeting was <u>interupted</u> by the unexpected arrival of the police.

85. "Although it is ultimately your choice, I would not <u>reccomend</u> the fish," advised Tim.

86. One saying that my mother frequently uses is 'Curiousity killed the cat!'.

87. Every week, the villagers offered up a <u>sacrafice</u> to appease the ogre who lived nearby.

88. We must do everything we can to eradicate all forms of <u>prejuidice</u> all over the world.

89. The weather in <u>Febuary</u> and March is usually appalling.

90. Billy <u>desprately</u> wanted to be asked to join his school's athletics team.

91. Several members of the <u>comittee</u> walked out of the meeting in disgust.

92. This sauce makes a delicious <u>accompniament</u> to these grilled scallops.

93. Toni and Raja had a fierce <u>arguement</u> over who should have more responsibility.

94. Henry the Eight and his daughter, Elizabeth the First, are extremely famous English monarchs.

95. Keyla is bilingual as she speaks two <u>langages</u> fluently: Portuguese and English.

96. "Such <u>occurences</u> are very rare in the animal kingdom," said the zoologist.

97. I think there has been a failure of <u>comunication</u> between voters and politicians.

98. Recycling is a crucial means by which we can help preserve the <u>enviroment</u>.

99. This figurine is just a replica; the <u>actuall</u> sculpture is over 6 metres tall.

100. In all <u>sinscerity</u>, I don't believe that Anna and Rita are the culprits this time.

**In each of the following, identify the words that are CORRECTLY spelt. Please note that, in some cases, you may need to select more than one option.**

_Examples:_

| | |
|---|---|
| ____ plate | ✓ handbag |
| ____ spoon | ____ handel |
| ____ fork | ✓ handwritten |
| ____ All 3 are incorrect | ____ All 3 are incorrect |
| ✓ All 3 are correct | ____ All 3 are correct |

101. ____ ancient
____ system
____ diligent
____ All 3 are incorrect
____ All 3 are correct

102. ____ agressive
____ shoulder
____ center
____ All 3 are incorrect
____ All 3 are correct

103. ____ knowledge
____ conveneience
____ ryhthym
____ All 3 are incorrect
____ All 3 are correct

104. ____ averrage
____ complete
____ acsidentally
____ All 3 are incorrect
____ All 3 are correct

105. ____ especialy
____ perculiar
____ continue
____ All 3 are incorrect
____ All 3 are correct

106. ____ existance
____ oppotunity
____ dettatched
____ All 3 are incorrect
____ All 3 are correct

107. ____ describe
____ equippment
____ frequently
____ All 3 are incorrect
____ All 3 are correct

108. ____ sincerley
____ posession
____ minuite
____ All 3 are incorrect
____ All 3 are correct

109. ____ experiement
____ expereince
____ expertise
____ All 3 are incorrect
____ All 3 are correct

110. ____ develop
____ soldier
____ posibble
____ All 3 are incorrect
____ All 3 are correct

111. ____ parallel
____ histry
____ garde
____ All 3 are incorrect
____ All 3 are correct

112. ____ noughty
____ material
____ fowards
____ All 3 are incorrect
____ All 3 are correct

113. ____ mention
____ bicycle
____ appear
____ All 3 are incorrect
____ All 3 are correct

114. ____ libray
____ extream
____ supose
____ All 3 are incorrect
____ All 3 are correct

115. ____ rhyme
____ lenght
____ thought
____ All 3 are incorrect
____ All 3 are correct

In each of the following, choose the pair of correctly spelt words that completes the given sentence. Indicate your choice by writing the appropriate letter (A, B, C, or D) in the box provided.

*Example:* **Bettina** _____ *a magic cloak which made her* _____ .

A. possessed ... invissible        C. possest ... invisable

B. posessed ... invisible          D. possessed ... invisible

| D |

116. The _____ was out of _____ because she had been running so hard.

A. women ... breathe        C. woman ... breathe

B. woman ... breath         D. womman ... breath

117. The _____ in our maths exam yesterday were more _____ than we expected.

A. qestions ... difificult      C. questions ... difficult

B. questcions ... dificult       D. questions ... difficulty

118. As the numbers of travellers _____, airports will become more _____.

A. increases ... busy        C. increase ... buzy

B. increses ... buisy         D. increase ... busy

119. If we _____ _____, we can get seats with a great view.

A. arrive ... early          C. arive ... earely

B. arrive ... earley         D. arrived ... earlie

120. Our _____ has _____ us a wonderful tour of Venice.

A. guide ... promissed       C. guide ... promised

B. giude ... prommised       D. guiude ... prommissed

121. Make sure you put _____ _____ on the wound to stop it bleeding.

A. enought ... presurre      C. enaugh ... pressure

B. enough ... pressure       D. enough ... pressur

122. The manager's _____ was pinned on the wall _____ the bathroom.

A. nottice ... oppossite      C. notice ... opposit

B. notise ... oppasite        D. notice ... opposite

123. The giant's _____ breathing was _____ interrupted by a few snores.

A. regular ... occasionally      C. regular ... occassionally

B. reguler ... ocassionally      D. regula ... occasionaly

124. The soldiers remained in their _____ even _____ they were terrified.

A. positions ... thought      C. positions ... though

B. positions ... thouhg       D. posicions ... through

Some of the following words are missing a hyphen. Write out each word in the space provided, inserting a hyphen where necessary.

*Examples:*         *deselect*              deselect

                    *coown*                 co-own

1.  reincarnation    _____

2.  coincide         _____

3.  antiinflammatory _____

4.  cooperation      _____

5.  reimburse        _____

6.  collaborate      _____

7.  deemphasise      _____

8.  deduce           _____

9.  antihero         _____

10. reemploy         _____

11. recurring        _____

12. semicircle       _____

13. reduce           _____

14. collision        _____

15. redeem           _____

# PREFIXES, VOWELS & HYPHENS

In each of the following, use an appropriate prefix from the Prefix Bank with the root word supplied in brackets to create a correctly spelt new word that sensibly completes each sentence. Be careful: some cases require a hyphen, while others do not.

**Example:** *As Jamila has changed her mind, we will have to _____ everything. (organise)*
*As Jamila has changed her mind, we will have to reorganise everything.*

**PREFIX BANK**

**co-    de-    re-    semi-    anti-    micro-**

16. Spacecraft become extremely hot when they _____ our atmosphere. (enter)

17. I have terrible hand-eye _____. (ordination)

18. The thieves used _____ weapons during the bank robbery. (automatic)

19. The engineers at Apple have _____ the iPhone's software. (designed)

20. Indira wants to become a _____ when she is older. (biologist)

21. Hopefully, this summit will help _____ the crisis. (escalate)

22. Your essay needs _____; it's still full of mistakes. (editing)

23. One way your body keeps you healthy is by producing _____. (bodies)

24. Gill and Richard are the _____ of the town gala. (organisers)

25. The _____ is a difficult punctuation mark to use. (colon)

26. The lieutenant was _____ because of his irresponsibility. (moted)

27. After 10 years, the police are _____ the unsolved case. (examining)

28. "Don't be _____, Pippa. Come and join us," her mother said. (social)

29. Mr Smith is hoping to be _____ as the leader of his party. (elected)

30. The elves had to _____ with the fairies to beat the goblins. (operate)

31. Bacteria are a type of _____. (organism)

11

In each of the following words, either the letters _ie_ or _ei_ have been removed. Decide which pair correctly completes each word, and then write the correctly spelt word in the space provided.

*Example:*   pr___st          _priest_

1.  fr____nd        _____

2.  l____sure        _____

3.  anx____ty        _____

4.  conven____nt     _____

5.  r____gn          _____

6.  fr____ght        _____

7.  for____gn        _____

8.  ____derdown      _____

9.  impat____nt      _____

10. br____fcase      _____

11. w____ght         _____

12. n____ghbourhood  _____

13. y____ld          _____

14. r____ndeer       _____

15. sover____gn      _____

16. hyg____ne        _____

17. gondol____r      _____

---

Show whether each sentence contains a spelling mistake or not. Use a tick to show the sentence is correct (☑) or a cross to show that it is not (☒).

_Examples:_   *The feild was full of sunflowers.*                                    ☒
              *There was a brief shocked silence before everyone started to argue.*   ☑

18.  You should always be quiet when you are in a library.                                  ☐

19.  We were all releived to discover that we had passed our exams.                         ☐

20.  Ibrahim saw an opportunity and siezed it with both hands.                              ☐

21.  The Roman army beseiged the town for months.                                          ☐

22.  The banks have warned us to be on the look-out for counterfeit money.                 ☐

23.  Kim's birthday is on the eighteenth of September.                                     ☐

24.  Surprisingly few people came to the unvieling of the town's new monument.             ☐

25.  Seaweed is an ingredeint that is commonly used in the Far East.                        ☐

26.  Dorothy grabbed the reins of her horse and vaulted into the saddle.                    ☐

27.  The headmaster was surprisingly leneint with the troublemakers.                        ☐

28.  All of the king's subjects grieved when he died.                                      ☐

29.  I don't know the difference between a brigadier and a leiutenant.                      ☐

30.  Pieces of glass fell off the chandeleir during the earthquake.                         ☐

31.  Some people believe that other planets are inhabited by aliens.                        ☐

32.  Fran's neice is a very disobedient child.                                             ☐

33.  The poltergeist made some extremely weird noises.                                      ☐

34.  The findings of the newest scientific report have not been well-recieved.              ☐

35.  Mrs Green likes drinking decaffeinated coffee in a biege mug.                          ☐

In each of the following, choose the pair of correctly spelt words that completes the given sentence. Indicate your choice by writing the appropriate letter (A, B, C, or D) in the box provided.

*Example:*    Jo's _____ is most _____ .

     A. *behaviour ... vexacious*      C. *behaviour ... vexatious*
     B. *behaiviour ... vexatious*      D. *behavior ... vexacious*

   **C**

1.   The _____ elf _____ forward carefully.
     A. cautious ... tiptoed        C. causious ... tiptoeded
     B. caucious ... tiptode        D. cuatious ... tiptoad

2.   The _____ wolves encircled the _____ deer.
     A. vitious ... defensless        C. vicious ... defenseless
     B. vitious ... deffenceless       D. vicious ... defenceless

3.   The honest _____ delivered the _____ cargo to the merchant.
     A. sailer ... pretious        C. saylor ... preshous
     B. sailor ... precious        D. sailor ... prescious

4.   _____ food doesn't have to be _____ .
     A. Nutricious ... inappetising     C. Newtritious ... unapettising
     B. Nutriscious ... inapettising     D. Nutritious ... unappetising

5.   The film we saw at the cinema was extremely _____ as it was very _____ .
     A. boring ... repetitious       C. borring ... repititious
     B. boreing ... repeticious       D. boring ... reppitious

6.   The story William told us was _____ ; it was utterly _____ .
     A. nonesense ... ficticious      C. nonsense ... fictitious
     B. nonesense ... fictitious      D. nonsense ... fictious

7.   The _____ scope of this novel makes it no less _____ .
     A. ambicious ... menotonous     C. ambitious ... monotinous
     B. ambitious ... monotonous     D. ambicious ... monotenous

8.   The ballroom was both _____ and _____ .
     A. spatious ... luxsurious      C. spacious ... luxurious
     B. spacious ... luxiurious      D. spatious ... luxorious

9.   Although Ingrid is a _____ reader, she is an _____ speller.
     A. veracious ... atrocious      C. voratious ... atrotious
     B. voracious ... atrotious      D. voracious ... atrocious

# -cious, -tious, & -ous  WORD ENDINGS

In each of the following, identify the words that are CORRECTLY spelt. Please note that, in some cases, you may need to select more than one option.

*Examples:*
- \_\_\_\_ plate
- \_\_\_\_ spoon
- \_\_\_\_ fork
- \_\_\_\_ All 3 are incorrect
- ✓ All 3 are correct

- ✓ handbag
- \_\_\_\_ handel
- ✓ handwritten
- \_\_\_\_ All 3 are incorrect
- \_\_\_\_ All 3 are correct

10. 
- \_\_\_ delitious
- \_\_\_ malitious
- \_\_\_ curious
- \_\_\_ All 3 are incorrect
- \_\_\_ All 3 are correct

11. 
- \_\_\_ famous
- \_\_\_ various
- \_\_\_ poisonous
- \_\_\_ All 3 are incorrect
- \_\_\_ All 3 are correct

12. 
- \_\_\_ anxious
- \_\_\_ suspicious
- \_\_\_ adventrous
- \_\_\_ All 3 are incorrect
- \_\_\_ All 3 are correct

13. 
- \_\_\_ superstitious
- \_\_\_ barbarious
- \_\_\_ hideous
- \_\_\_ All 3 are incorrect
- \_\_\_ All 3 are correct

14. 
- \_\_\_ mountanous
- \_\_\_ dangerous
- \_\_\_ perilous
- \_\_\_ All 3 are incorrect
- \_\_\_ All 3 are correct

15. 
- \_\_\_ humungous
- \_\_\_ conscious
- \_\_\_ hazzardous
- \_\_\_ All 3 are incorrect
- \_\_\_ All 3 are correct

16. 
- \_\_\_ in-famous
- \_\_\_ lushous
- \_\_\_ marvelous
- \_\_\_ All 3 are incorrect
- \_\_\_ All 3 are correct

17. 
- \_\_\_ tremendous
- \_\_\_ outragious
- \_\_\_ jealous
- \_\_\_ All 3 are incorrect
- \_\_\_ All 3 are correct

18. 
- \_\_\_ precarious
- \_\_\_ precipitous
- \_\_\_ precocious
- \_\_\_ All 3 are incorrect
- \_\_\_ All 3 are correct

19. 
- \_\_\_ tedious
- \_\_\_ joyous
- \_\_\_ glamarous
- \_\_\_ All 3 are incorrect
- \_\_\_ All 3 are correct

20. 
- \_\_\_ gracious
- \_\_\_ infectious
- \_\_\_ anonymous
- \_\_\_ All 3 are incorrect
- \_\_\_ All 3 are correct

21. 
- \_\_\_ vigourous
- \_\_\_ trecherous
- \_\_\_ venomous
- \_\_\_ All 3 are incorrect
- \_\_\_ All 3 are correct

22. 
- \_\_\_ ridiculous
- \_\_\_ thundrous
- \_\_\_ herbiverous
- \_\_\_ All 3 are incorrect
- \_\_\_ All 3 are correct

23. 
- \_\_\_ fabbulous
- \_\_\_ disasterous
- \_\_\_ pretencious
- \_\_\_ All 3 are incorrect
- \_\_\_ All 3 are correct

24. 
- \_\_\_ prosprous
- \_\_\_ rebbelious
- \_\_\_ stuppendous
- \_\_\_ All 3 are incorrect
- \_\_\_ All 3 are correct

For each of the following, select the one correct spelling from the choices given.

*Example:*  *The only piece of evidence the police had was _____.*

A.  *circumstancial*      B.  *circamstantial*      (C.)  *circumstantial*      D.  *circumstantiall*

1.  Learning to spell well is an _____ skill.
    A.  essential          B.  essencial          C.  essenntial          D.  essenncial

2.  You can't read that letter; it's _____!
    A.  confedential      B.  confidencial      C.  confidential      D.  confiddential

3.  Lots of _____ ingredients are bad for us.
    A.  artifitial          B.  arteficial          C.  artifiscial          D.  artificial

4.  Many important _____ attended the meeting with the Prime Minister.
    A.  officials          B.  offitials          C.  oficcials          D.  ofiscials

5.  The shepherd had a very _____ accent.
    A.  provintial          B.  provincial          C.  provinncial          D.  provential

6.  The children had prepared a _____ surprise for their mother's birthday.
    A.  spescial          B.  speciel          C.  special          D.  speicial

7.  We live in a quiet, _____ area.
    A.  resedential          B.  residencial          C.  residential          D.  resedencial

8.  The unfeeling stepmother gave the child a _____ stare.
    A.  glacial          B.  glasial          C.  glatial          D.  galacial

9.  Many young people nowadays get their news from _____ media.
    A.  soscial          B.  soccial          C.  sotial          D.  social

10. Today, we watched several interesting _____.
    A.  infommercials      B.  infomercials      C.  infomertials      D.  informmertials

All of the following words end with either the letters -cial or -tial. Use the clues given to help you work out what each word is. Then, fill in the missing letters of the word so that it is spelt correctly.

*Example:*  *First*  i n _ _ _ _ l

*First*  i n i t i a l

11. On the surface  s ___ p ___ ___ f ___ ___ ___ ___ ___

12. Relating to money  f ___ n ___ n ___ ___ ___ ___

13. A bit of something  p ___ r ___ ___ ___ ___

14. Relating to trade  c o m ___ ___ ___ ___ ___ ___ ___

15. Possible  p ___ t ___ ___ ___ ___ ___ ___

16. In order  s ___ q u ___ n ___ ___ ___ ___

17. Relating to race  r ___ ___ ___ ___ ___

18. Like a palace  p ___ l ___ ___ ___ ___ ___

19. Very important  c r ___ ___ ___ ___ ___

20. Having influence  i ___ f l ___ ___ ___ ___ ___ ___ ___

21. Particular  e s p ___ ___ ___ ___ ___

22. Relating to war  m a ___ ___ ___ ___ ___

23. Unbiased; fair  i m p ___ ___ ___ ___ ___ ___

24. Relating to the face  f ___ ___ ___ ___ ___

25. Not authorized  u n o ___ ___ ___ ___ ___ ___ ___

26. Having good results  b ___ n ___ f ___ ___ ___ ___ ___

27. Relating to a judge  j ___ d ___ ___ ___ ___ ___

28. Of real value  s ___ b s ___ ___ ___ ___ ___ ___ ___

See how well you remember the spellings of the words in Units 1-5! In all of the following tests, show whether each word is correct or incorrect.

*Examples:*     *hello*         ☑

                    *wellcome*     ☒

## TEST 6.1

1. accident ☐
2. awkword ☐
3. barbrous ☐
4. calendar ☐
5. compleat ☐
6. de-duce ☐
7. excellant ☐
8. greived ☐
9. jealous ☐
10. martial ☐
11. occassion ☐
12. parallel ☐
13. pressure ☐
14. quiet ☐
15. sacrafice ☐
16. suspitious ☐
17. twelth ☐
18. unofficial ☐
19. variaty ☐
20. weight ☐

SCORE _____ /20

## TEST 6.2

1. acompany ☐
2. averrage ☐
3. beige ☐
4. category ☐
5. confidencial ☐
6. de-emphasise ☐
7. exerscise ☐
8. glamorous ☐
9. impartial ☐
10. mallicious ☐
11. occupy ☐
12. particuler ☐
13. potential ☐
14. relevent ☐
15. redeam ☐
16. sceintific ☐
17. supprise ☐
18. suppose ☐
19. tremmendous ☐
20. vigerous ☐

SCORE _____ /20

## TEST 6.3

1. adventureous ☐
2. arrive ☐
3. beleive ☐
4. cautious ☐
5. curriosity ☐
6. desparate ☐
7. eighteenth ☐
8. Februray ☐
9. glacial ☐
10. impatiant ☐
11. length ☐
12. mention ☐
13. neice ☐
14. officials ☐
15. physical ☐
16. prescious ☐
17. residential ☐
18. redeseigned ☐
19. sincere ☐
20. wierd ☐

SCORE _____ /20

## TEST 6.4

1. aliens ☐
2. anxiety ☐
3. benificial ☐
4. century ☐
5. controvasy ☐
6. dictionary ☐
7. especiall ☐
8. favourate ☐
9. gondolier ☐
10. harrassed ☐
11. increase ☐
12. leisure ☐
13. microbiolagist ☐
14. nutricious ☐
15. opposite ☐
16. pieces ☐
17. prosprous ☐
18. reduce ☐
19. re-elected ☐
20. semiautomatic ☐
21. superfficial ☐
22. vennomous ☐

SCORE _____ /22

## TEST 6.5

1. ambicious ☐
2. arguement ☐
3. beseiged ☐
4. chandelier ☐
5. convienience ☐
6. dissappear ☐
7. existance ☐
8. facial ☐
9. hazadous ☐
10. infammous ☐
11. library ☐
12. marvellous ☐
13. ordinery ☐
14. poisonous ☐
15. purpose ☐
16. recent ☐
17. re-employ ☐
18. semicircle ☐
19. soveriegn ☐
20. tedious ☐
21. unveilling ☐
22. well-recieved ☐

SCORE _____ /22

## TEST 6.6

1. antibodies ☐
2. atroscious ☐
3. bicycle ☐
4. co-incide ☐
5. co-operate ☐
6. died ☐
7. experiment ☐
8. finnancial ☐
9. herbiverous ☐
10. infectious ☐
11. lenient ☐
12. leiutenant ☐
13. minuite ☐
14. possesion ☐
15. quarter ☐
16. ryhthm ☐
17. reenter ☐
18. regular ☐
19. racial ☐
20. seized ☐
21. superstious ☐
22. vicious ☐

SCORE _____ /22

## TEST 6.7

1. ammateur ☐
2. artiffical ☐
3. breathe ☐
4. collaborrate ☐
5. coordinaition ☐
6. deliscious ☐
7. extreame ☐
8. essential ☐
9. fictitous ☐
10. hiddeous ☐
11. influential ☐
12. knowledge ☐
13. luscious ☐
14. microorganism ☐
15. notice ☐
16. outragious ☐
17. partial ☐
18. possible ☐
19. reins ☐
20. remember ☐
21. speciall ☐
22. unappettising ☐

## TEST 6.8

1. address ☐
2. appear ☐
3. briefcase ☐
4. collision ☐
5. counterfiet ☐
6. desperetely ☐
7. experience ☐
8. eigth ☐
9. forewards ☐
10. humungous ☐
11. info-mercials ☐
12. luxiurious ☐
13. mountanous ☐
14. perculiar ☐
15. prejudice ☐
16. queue ☐
17. relieved ☐
18. repeticious ☐
19. sinscerely ☐
20. signiture ☐
21. tomorow ☐
22. various ☐

## TEST 6.9

1. antiheroe ☐
2. anxious ☐
3. briggadier ☐
4. commercial ☐
5. conssious ☐
6. disasterous ☐
7. equippment ☐
8. especialy ☐
9. foreign ☐
10. goverment ☐
11. hygeine ☐
12. ingredeient ☐
13. naughty ☐
14. opportunity ☐
15. perillous ☐
16. provincial ☐
17. ryhyme ☐
18. restaraunt ☐
19. re-examinning ☐
20. secratary ☐
21. social ☐
22. thundrous ☐

SCORE _____ /22

SCORE _____ /22

SCORE _____ /22

## TEST 6.10

1. acciddentally ☐
2. agressive ☐
3. brusied ☐
4. comittee ☐
5. co-organisers ☐
6. criticises ☐
7. determinacion ☐
8. enviroment ☐
9. explaination ☐
10. friend ☐
11. gracious ☐
12. neccessary ☐
13. palatial ☐
14. programe ☐
15. reccurring ☐
16. reigndeer ☐
17. ridiculous ☐
18. spatious ☐
19. substancial ☐
20. sentence ☐
21. therefor ☐
22. Wendnesday ☐

SCORE _____ /22

## TEST 6.11

1. accompianment ☐
2. anonymous ☐
3. communication ☐
4. co-operation ☐
5. crucial ☐
6. demmoted ☐
7. disobiedient ☐
8. embarass ☐
9. frequently ☐
10. grammer ☐
11. monotonous ☐
12. occurences ☐
13. parlament ☐
14. pretensious ☐
15. recomend ☐
16. re-editing ☐
17. reign ☐
18. semicollon ☐
19. sequential ☐
20. sinscerity ☐
21. tempareture ☐
22. yeild ☐

SCORE _____ /22

## TEST 6.12

1. anti-inflamatory ☐
2. antisocial ☐
3. competition ☐
4. conveinient ☐
5. curious ☐
6. decafeinated ☐
7. de-escalated ☐
8. eiderdown ☐
9. expertise ☐
10. freight ☐
11. guarrantee ☐
12. judicial ☐
13. neighborhood ☐
14. ocassionally ☐
15. poltergiest ☐
16. pronounciation ☐
17. reincarnation ☐
18. rebelious ☐
19. reimburse ☐
20. stupendous ☐
21. trecherous ☐
22. voracious ☐

SCORE _____ /22

Complete the following statements using the prefix <u>dis-</u>, <u>mis-</u>, <u>il-</u>, or <u>ir-</u>. Then write the correctly spelt word in the space provided.

*Example:* _____ + *take* ⇨ _____

_____ <u>mis</u> + *take* ⇨ _____<u>mistake</u>_____

1. _____ + courage ⇨ _____

2. _____ + lead ⇨ _____

3. _____ + relevant ⇨ _____

4. _____ + behave ⇨ _____

5. _____ + possess ⇨ _____

6. _____ + print ⇨ _____

7. _____ + address ⇨ _____

8. _____ + regular ⇨ _____

9. _____ + obey ⇨ _____

10. _____ + govern ⇨ _____

11. _____ + legal ⇨ _____

12. _____ + count ⇨ _____

13. _____ + agree ⇨ _____

14. _____ + guide ⇨ _____

15. _____ + heard ⇨ _____

16. _____ + appoint ⇨ _____

17. _____ + legible ⇨ _____

18. _____ + rational ⇨ _____

19. _____ + allow ⇨ _____

20. _____ + regard ⇨ _____

21. _____ + pose ⇨ _____

22. _____ + fit ⇨ _____

23. _____ + shaped ⇨ _____

24. _____ + arm ⇨ _____

25. _____ + able ⇨ _____

26. _____ + align ⇨ _____

27. _____ + conduct ⇨ _____

28. _____ + card ⇨ _____

29. _____ + grace ⇨ _____

30. _____ + honest ⇨ _____

31. _____ + handle ⇨ _____

32. _____ + label ⇨ _____

# dis-, mis-, il-, & ir- PREFIXES

---

NONE of the following words have been spelt correctly. Write the correct spelling of each word in the space provided.

33. ilitterate _____

34. disaproval _____

35. mispelled _____

36. iresponsible _____

37. dissapearence _____

38. misremmember _____

39. disatisfied _____

40. discontinueing _____

41. mistreatmant _____

42. disadvantege _____

43. disaggreeible _____

44. ilogicall _____

45. mistrustfull _____

46. irrisitible _____

47. dissapointmant _____

48. misaprehention _____

49. misdead _____

50. irreversable _____

51. mislayd _____

52. disembarcked _____

53. discourtious _____

54. misdirrection _____

55. disasembile _____

56. discomfurt _____

57. misinfomation _____

58. disinchanted _____

59. misconseption _____

60. disimilarity _____

61. misaplied _____

62. disrupcion _____

63. mispeak _____

64. disordaly _____

65. misjudgded _____

66. dismissel _____

67. illegitemate _____

68. disbeleivingly _____

23

> In each of the following, show whether the given word is spelt correctly or incorrectly. If the word is incorrectly spelt, write the correct spelling in the space provided.
>
> **_Examples:_**  ancient  ☑  _____
>
> neice  ☒  _niece_

1.  concieve  ☐  _____
2.  mischeivous  ☐  _____
3.  conscience  ☐  _____
4.  species  ☐  _____
5.  cieling  ☐  _____
6.  achievement  ☐  _____
7.  nuclei  ☐  _____
8.  societies  ☐  _____
9.  juciest  ☐  _____
10.  conceirge  ☐  _____
11.  piecemeal  ☐  _____
12.  reicipts  ☐  _____
13.  glacier  ☐  _____
14.  financeir  ☐  _____
15.  peircingly  ☐  _____
16.  deceivers  ☐  _____
17.  recipies  ☐  _____
18.  deficiency  ☐  _____
19.  omniscient  ☐  _____
20.  transcievers  ☐  _____
21.  concietedness  ☐  _____
22.  unperceived  ☐  _____

---

> Many of the following words have Greek or Latin origins. Carefully read the words in each group, then answer the question beneath them. Write your answer in the space provided.
>
> _**Example:**_ _science   discipline   inescapable   ascend_
> _**In which word are the letters 'sc' pronounced differently?**_     _inescapable_

1. scheme  chorus  charity  anarchy
   In which word are the letters 'ch' pronounced differently? _____

2. crypt  calypso  lyric  psyche
   In which word is the letter 'y' pronounced differently? _____

3. mascot  crescent  cascade  fiasco
   In which word are the letters 'sc' pronounced differently? _____

4. cyanide  photosynthesis  syndicate  synonym
   In which word is the letter 'y' pronounced differently? _____

5. Achilles  bronchitis  enchilada  monarchy
   In which word are the letters 'ch' pronounced differently? _____

6. symbol  rye  typical  symptom
   In which word is the letter 'y' pronounced differently? _____

7. martyr  sty  pyre  typhoon
   In which word is the letter 'y' pronounced differently? _____

8. obscene  adolescent  scimitar  crescendo
   In which word are the letters 'sc' pronounced differently? _____

9. chided  urchins  archipelago  besmirched
   In which word are the letters 'ch' pronounced differently? _____

10. gymkhana  gyroscope  hymn  gymnasium
    In which word is the letter 'y' pronounced differently? _____

11. hibiscus  escapade  fresco  fluorescent
    In which word are the letters 'sc' pronounced differently? _____

> Each underlined word below has either a Greek or Latin origin. Show whether each underlined word is spelt correctly or not. Use a tick to show the word is correct (☑) or a cross to show that it is not (☒).
>
> _**Examples:**_    _The ship's <u>anchor</u> was covered with barnacles._      ☑
>
>                _Google <u>Crome</u> is the name of a very popular web browser._      ☒

12. Although the portrait was <u>asymetrical</u>, it was still beautiful to look at. ☐

13. The politician was extremely popular because she was so <u>charismatic</u>. ☐

14. The rebels' <u>scheames</u> were discovered by the king's spies. ☐

15. Two sides of an <u>isosseles</u> triangle are equal in length. ☐

16. Car drivers should always be aware that there may be <u>cyclists</u> on the road. ☐

17. Penny went to a concert with her mother to hear a famous <u>orchestra</u> play. ☐

18. The strange noise kept <u>ecchoing</u> around the vast cave. ☐

19. <u>Crysanthemums</u> are among my favourite flowers. ☐

20. Our class went to see a play with wonderful <u>scenary</u> at the Old Vic. ☐

21. The duck-billed <u>platipus</u> is an interesting, but peculiar, semi-aquatic creature. ☐

22. Although many children love <u>effervescent</u> drinks, they are usually full of sugar. ☐

23. The famous Pyramid of Djoser was designed by Imhotep, the <u>arcitecht</u>. ☐

24. I have always been <u>suseptible</u> to headaches. ☐

25. Holding his <u>scepter</u> aloft, the emperor declared the start of the Games. ☐

26. The eyes of the <u>chameleon</u> can move in different directions at the same time. ☐

27. Gerhardt decided that he wanted to learn how to play the <u>tympani</u>. ☐

28. A suspicious-looking <u>character</u> was loitering in the park, so Ida called the police. ☐

29. Desiderius Erasmus was a famous Dutch <u>scolar</u> who was born in 1466. ☐

30. Historians used to believe that medieval society was exceedingly <u>heirarchical</u>. ☐

# WORDS FROM OTHER LANGUAGES

UNIT 9

One word in each of the following sentences is a word of French origin that is missing a letter string. Read the sentence carefully to work out what the word is. Then, fill in the missing letters so that the word is spelt correctly.

*Example:* **Amanda made us a delicious q_____e for supper.**
*Amanda made us a delicious quiche for supper.*

31. The restaurant's fabulous new c_____f is Italian.

32. The rude boy stuck out his t_____e at the kindly old man.

33. The pantomime villain had a huge beard and a twirly m_____e.

34. This sculpture is u_____e; there isn't another one like it in the world.

35. Our washing m_____e has broken down again.

36. Hal has become a member of the Essex Junior Football L_____e.

37. Jamie received a holiday b_____e from Thomas Cook.

38. The skydiver opened her p_____e after she jumped out of the aeroplane.

39. Last summer, Ivan spent a month in a c_____t in Switzerland.

40. Jamila has an a_____e bowl that is over two hundred years old.

41. The manager thanked all of his c_____s for their hard work.

42. Kelly's b_____e sells a collection of vintage and second-hand clothes.

43. The Black Death is the name of a deadly fourteenth-century p_____e.

44. King Arthur's knights were famous for their c_____y.

45. Mark bought Tiffany a beautiful b_____t of flowers for her birthday.

46. Hanging from the ceiling was a wonderful crystal c_____r.

47. We will send you our monthly c_____e full of our latest products.

48. Liam is allergic to p_____o nuts.

49. Ahmed went to the bank to cash the c_____e his uncle had given him.

27

> Many of the following words have French origins. Carefully read the words in each group, then answer the question beneath them. Write your answer in the space provided.
>
> _**Example:**_   _delinquent   conquer   squelch   queen_
>           _**In which word are the letters 'que' pronounced differently?**_      _conquer_

50. picturesque   consequence   quest   squeak
    In which word are the letters 'que' pronounced differently?     _____

51. bewitch   challenge   archer   champagne
    In which word are the letters 'ch' pronounced differently?     _____

52. banquet   racquet   prequel   squelch
    In which word are the letters 'que' pronounced differently?     _____

53. query   aqueduct   physique   queasy
    In which word are the letters 'que' pronounced differently?     _____

54. orchid   chlorine   stomach   fuchsia
    In which word are the letters 'ch' pronounced differently?     _____

55. request   grotesque   squeeze   frequent
    In which word are the letters 'que' pronounced differently?     _____

56. arachnid   chaperone   machete   chivalrous
    In which word are the letters 'ch' pronounced differently?     _____

57. technique   mosque   question   plaque
    In which word are the letters 'que' pronounced differently?     _____

58. avalanche   crochet   crèche   archive
    In which word are the letters 'ch' pronounced differently?     _____

59. chic   chasm   chauffeur   charade
    In which word are the letters 'ch' pronounced differently?     _____

60. bequeath   equestrian   querulous   opaque
    In which word are the letters 'que' pronounced differently?     _____

In each of the following, add the word ending **-ly** or **-ally** to each root word given in brackets. Make any necessary changes, then use the correctly spelt word to complete the sentence.

*Example:* *"I think I have done very _____ in my exam," moaned Rita. (bad)*
*"I think I have done very <u>badly</u> in my exam," moaned Rita. (bad)*

1.  The politicians were all _____ elected. (democratic)

2.  The twins, Jo and Kit, went to the party _____. (separate)

3.  You shouldn't judge other people too _____. (harsh)

4.  The old man shook his head _____ at the foolish knight. (grave)

5.  _____, Samantha agreed to help clean the kitchen. (begrudging)

6.  "Don't take Bob too _____," Dot advised Nina. (literal)

7.  As the phone was made so _____, it broke very quickly. (flimsy)

8.  The Fairy Queen _____ made us disappear. (magic)

9.  He believed_____ that everything was going to be fine. (naive)

10. Tim argued_____ that he should be given a new X-Box. (persuasive)

11. "Such behaviour is _____ unacceptable!" said Gina. (complete)

12. The fans behaved _____ when their team lost. (abominable)

13. The clients_____ agreed to the terms of the contract. (ready)

14. _____ speaking, that is not true at all. (historic)

15. _____, I go to bed at 11 pm. (ordinary)

16. "I will meet you at six o'clock _____," he promised. (precise)

17. "The worm will return," Sherlock Holmes said _____. (cryptic)

18. "Help...me," whispered the wounded soldier _____. (hoarse)

19. All our products are _____ friendly. (environment)

In each of the following, you are given the definition of a word. Select the one correct spelling of the word that is being defined from the choices given.

*Example:*  *In a fitting, or an appropriate, manner*

    **A.**   *suitabley*      **B.**   *suitibly*      **C.**   *suitabally*      **(D.)**   *suitably*

20.  In a very sad, depressed, or despondent way
    A.  misrabaly    B.  misarebly    C.  misrebly    D.  miserably

21.  In an uncomplicated or simple way
    A.  basicly    B.  basically    C.  basiscaly    D.  basecly

22.  In an instantaneous manner
    A.  immediatley    B.  immediatly    C.  immediately    D.  immedietley

23.  In a happy way
    A.  cheerily    B.  cheeryly    C.  cheerilly    D.  cheerally

24.  In a manner that cannot be explained
    A.  inexplicabally    B.  inexplicibly    C.  inexplicably    D.  inexplicabably

25.  In a solemn and self-important manner
    A.  pomposly    B.  pompusally    C.  pompusly    D.  pompously

26.  In a scholarly way or fashion
    A.  academicly    B.  academically    C.  accademically    D.  accademicly

27.  In a way that only lasts for a limited period of time
    A.  temporarally    B.  temperarily    C.  temperarally    D.  temporarily

28.  In a material, definite, or real way
    A.  tangibly    B.  tangeably    C.  tangibally    D.  tangebally

29.  In a complex or complicated way
    A.  elabourately    B.  elaboratly    C.  elaborately    D.  elaborateley

# -able, -ible, -ably, & -ibly  WORD ENDINGS          UNIT 11

Complete the following statements using either the suffix -able or -ible. Then write the correctly spelt word — having made any necessary changes — in the space provided.

Examples:  reason + ___ ⇨ _____        reduce + ___ ⇨ _____

reason + able ⇨ reasonable           reduce + ible ⇨ reducible

1.  prevent + _____ ⇨ _____
2.  envy + _____ ⇨ _____
3.  apply + _____ ⇨ _____
4.  mention + _____ ⇨ _____
5.  adore + _____ ⇨ _____
6.  question + _____ ⇨ _____
7.  admit + _____ ⇨ _____
8.  reverse + _____ ⇨ _____
9.  like + _____ ⇨ _____
10. answer + _____ ⇨ _____
11. construct + _____ ⇨ _____
12. imagine + _____ ⇨ _____
13. deny + _____ ⇨ _____
14. attach + _____ ⇨ _____
15. deduce + _____ ⇨ _____
16. regret + _____ ⇨ _____

17. knowledge + _____ ⇨ _____
18. recommend + _____ ⇨ _____
19. programme + _____ ⇨ _____
20. achieve + _____ ⇨ _____
21. vary + _____ ⇨ _____
22. access + _____ ⇨ _____
23. breathe + _____ ⇨ _____
24. suggest + _____ ⇨ _____
25. collapse + _____ ⇨ _____
26. destruct + _____ ⇨ _____
27. tolerate + _____ ⇨ _____
28. suppose + _____ ⇨ _____
29. divide + _____ ⇨ _____
30. consume + _____ ⇨ _____
31. collect + _____ ⇨ _____
32. appreciate + _____ ⇨ _____

In each of the following, choose the pair of correctly spelt words that completes the given sentence. Indicate your choice by writing the appropriate letter (A, B, C, or D) in the box provided.

*Example:*  That _____ is _____ .

    A. materiall ... flamable
    B. material ... flammable

    C. matterial ... flamible
    D. meterial ... flamable

    B

33.  The _____ Hilda reached was highly _____ .
    A. conclusion ... debatible
    B. conclucion ... debatably
    C. conclusion ... debatable
    D. conclution ... dibatable

34.  The _____ caused by the tropical storm was _____ greater than we thought.
    A. dammage ... consideribly
    B. damage ... considerably
    C. dammige ... considerabley
    D. damadge ... considrably

35.  For once, the _____ put forward by Mandy was _____ made.
    A. suggestian ... sensibley
    B. sugestion ... sensably
    C. suggestion ... senseabley
    D. suggestion ... sensibly

36.  That chair is not particularly _____ ; I think we should _____ a new one.
    A. comfortable ... purchase
    B. comftable ... perchase
    C. comfortible ... purchous
    D. comftible ... purchase

37.  The handwriting in the book was barely _____ ; it was almost _____ to read.
    A. leggible ... impossable
    B. legiable ... impossible
    C. legable ... impposssible
    D. legible ... impossible

38.  The weather has not been _____ recently; it's been extremely _____ .
    A. reliable ... changable
    B. reliable ... changeable
    C. relyible ... changible
    D. relyable ... changeable

39.  Brutus' speech was a _____ reminder of how _____ people could be.
    A. forceable ... pesuadable
    B. forceible ... persuadible
    C. forcible ... persuadable
    D. forcibel ... persuadeible

40.  My favourite TV series is _____ _____ ; every episode is always entertaining.
    A. dependibly ... enjoyible
    B. dependabley ... injoyable
    C. dependably ... enjoyable
    D. dipendably ... enjoiable

41.  Martin's behaviour has changed _____ , which is completely _____ .
    A. noticeably ... understandable
    B. notibly ... understandable
    C. noticeably ... understandible
    D. noticably ... understandable

See how well you remember the correct spellings of the words in Units 7-11! In all of the following tests, show whether each word is correct or incorrect.

**Examples:**
| hello | ☑ |
|---|---|
| wellcome | ☒ |

## TEST 12.1

1. acheivable ☐
2. architect ☐
3. basically ☐
4. cheerily ☐
5. crypt ☐
6. colleaugues ☐
7. dissable ☐
8. discount ☐
9. elabourately ☐
10. grave ☐
11. hoarse ☐
12. imediately ☐
13. juicest ☐
14. literral ☐
15. magic ☐
16. misaddress ☐
17. misconduct ☐
18. precise ☐
19. physique ☐
20. ready ☐

## TEST 12.2

1. accessable ☐
2. archive ☐
3. bancquet ☐
4. complete ☐
5. consequence ☐
6. champaigne ☐
7. disaggree ☐
8. discouradge ☐
9. frequent ☐
10. glacier ☐
11. harsh ☐
12. imaginable ☐
13. ill-logical ☐
14. misalign ☐
15. mischievious ☐
16. misdirection ☐
17. naive ☐
18. pesuasive ☐
19. raquet ☐
20. scepter ☐

## TEST 12.3

1. abhominable ☐
2. begrudgeing ☐
3. concieve ☐
4. collectibal ☐
5. chandalier ☐
6. chasm ☐
7. disallow ☐
8. dissappoint ☐
9. disgrace ☐
10. finnancier ☐
11. historic ☐
12. ir-rational ☐
13. leaugue ☐
14. missfit ☐
15. mispelt ☐
16. miseribly ☐
17. ordinary ☐
18. pierceingly ☐
19. parashute ☐
20. request ☐

SCORE _____ /20

SCORE _____ /20

SCORE _____ /20

## TEST 12.4

1. academically ☐
2. avalanch ☐
3. boutique ☐
4. constructible ☐
5. chorous ☐
6. charactar ☐
7. decievers ☐
8. dissapearance ☐
9. dishonest ☐
10. enjoyible ☐
11. fiasco ☐
12. irregular ☐
13. legible ☐
14. missapplied ☐
15. mentionible ☐
16. mishandle ☐
17. plauge ☐
18. receipts ☐
19. scheame ☐
20. squeltch ☐
21. tollerable ☐
22. typical ☐

SCORE _____ /22

## TEST 12.5

1. admissable ☐
2. attachable ☐
3. consummable ☐
4. cascade ☐
5. chameleon ☐
6. deduceable ☐
7. dissaproval ☐
8. disobey ☐
9. flimsy ☐
10. gymmasium ☐
11. inexpliccably ☐
12. misbehave ☐
13. misinfomation ☐
14. mislayed ☐
15. mispeak ☐
16. persuasively ☐
17. quest ☐
18. regretable ☐
19. societys ☐
20. symbol ☐
21. scholar ☐
22. scenary ☐

SCORE _____ /22

## TEST 12.6

1. adoreable ☐
2. aprecciate ☐
3. cryptical ☐
4. comfortible ☐
5. ceiling ☐
6. demacratic ☐
7. dissasemble ☐
8. dispose ☐
9. environment ☐
10. hymn ☐
11. impossible ☐
12. iliterate ☐
13. likeable ☐
14. misconception ☐
15. misjudged ☐
16. piecemeal ☐
17. picturesque ☐
18. readilly ☐
19. sepparate ☐
20. suggestion ☐
21. synonnym ☐
22. transcievers ☐

SCORE _____ /22

## TEST 12.7

1. answerable ☐
2. acqueduct ☐
3. collapsable ☐
4. concsience ☐
5. chaperrone ☐
6. denible ☐
7. dissmisal ☐
8. disorderly ☐
9. forcible ☐
10. gravely ☐
11. iresponsible ☐
12. magically ☐
13. misgovern ☐
14. moustasche ☐
15. mishaped ☐
16. platypus ☐
17. persuadible ☐
18. query ☐
19. reliable ☐
20. suppossable ☐
21. symptom ☐
22. tangeably ☐

SCORE _____ /22

## TEST 12.8

1. appliccable ☐
2. anarchy ☐
3. conceierge ☐
4. changeable ☐
5. carismatic ☐
6. destructable ☐
7. disregard ☐
8. enviable ☐
9. harshly ☐
10. irrellevant ☐
11. knowledgable ☐
12. misheard ☐
13. nuclei ☐
14. ordinarily ☐
15. preventible ☐
16. pompously ☐
17. recommendible ☐
18. species ☐
19. technicque ☐
20. typhoon ☐
21. temporrarily ☐
22. understandable ☐

SCORE _____ /22

## TEST 12.9

1. apprecible ☐
2. asymmetrical ☐
3. brochure ☐
4. conclusion ☐
5. checque ☐
6. chaffeur ☐
7. dissapointment ☐
8. disruption ☐
9. divisable ☐
10. fluourescent ☐
11. gyrascope ☐
12. irrisistible ☐
13. ilegall ☐
14. lyric ☐
15. mistrustfull ☐
16. misguide ☐
17. precisely ☐
18. placque ☐
19. senseably ☐
20. tympany ☐
21. unperceivied ☐
22. variable ☐

SCORE _____ /22

## TEST 12.10

1. achievement ☐
2. bouquet ☐
3. chivalrous ☐
4. cryptic ☐
5. consideribly ☐
6. charade ☐
7. dammage ☐
8. defieciency ☐
9. disbelievingly ☐
10. disposess ☐
11. environmentally ☐
12. flimsily ☐
13. historicly ☐
14. ireversible ☐
15. literally ☐
16. misspelled ☐
17. noticeably ☐
18. orchid ☐
19. programable ☐
20. psychye ☐
21. recipies ☐
22. separately ☐

SCORE _____ /22

## TEST 12.11

1. adolescent ☐
2. bronchittis ☐
3. catologue ☐
4. completely ☐
5. crescent ☐
6. debatible ☐
7. democratically ☐
8. discontinueing ☐
9. disenchanted ☐
10. dissatissfied ☐
11. ecquestrian ☐
12. grotesque ☐
13. hoarsley ☐
14. ilegitimate ☐
15. mistreatment ☐
16. opaque ☐
17. pistacchio ☐
18. purchase ☐
19. queazy ☐
20. reversable ☐
21. synddicate ☐
22. suggestable ☐

SCORE _____ /22

## TEST 12.12

1. abominabley ☐
2. begrudgingly ☐
3. chrysanthmums ☐
4. concietedness ☐
5. crèeche ☐
6. deppendably ☐
7. disadvantadge ☐
8. disagreable ☐
9. discourteous ☐
10. disembarcked ☐
11. disimilarity ☐
12. effevescent ☐
13. gymkana ☐
14. hierarchical ☐
15. isosceles ☐
16. ill-legible ☐
17. matyr ☐
18. missapprehension ☐
19. naiively ☐
20. omniescient ☐
21. photosynethesis ☐
22. questionable ☐

SCORE _____ /22

> Complete the following sentences by adding either the prefix <u>im-</u> or <u>in-</u> to each of the given words to form a word that has the OPPOSITE meaning to the given word.
>
> _**Example:**_  _**The opposite of perfect is**_ _____ .
> _The opposite of perfect is <u>imperfect</u>._

1.  The opposite of **mature** is _____ .

2.  The opposite of **attentive** is _____ .

3.  The opposite of **correct** is _____ .

4.  The opposite of **balance** is _____ .

5.  The opposite of **advisable** is _____ .

6.  The opposite of **mortal** is _____ .

7.  The opposite of **patient** is _____ .

8.  The opposite of **definite** is _____ .

9.  The opposite of **prudent** is _____ .

10.  The opposite of **famous** is _____ .

11.  The opposite of **adequate** is _____ .

12.  The opposite of **practical** is _____ .

13.  The opposite of **sufficient** is _____ .

14.  The opposite of **precise** is _____ .

15.  The opposite of **justice** is _____ .

16.  The opposite of **valid** is _____ .

17.  The opposite of **moral** is _____ .

18.  The opposite of **edible** is _____ .

19.  The opposite of **moveable** is _____ .

In each of the following, select the prefix that creates a correctly spelt word which sensibly completes each sentence.

*Example:*  Make sure you do not (in / re / im)pose on people's generosity.

Make sure you do not (in / re / *im*)pose on people's generosity.

20.  No decisions can be made until we (inter / re / in)view the results of the experiment.

21.  It's surprising how many people choose to (inter / re / im)migrate each year.

22.  Rewrite the following sentences as (in / re / im)direct speech.

23.  It will cost a fortune to (im / in / re)novate that nineteenth-century building.

24.  Kim only (in / im / re)plied that she would come; she never gave us a definite answer.

25.  Our school has a yearly (inter / re / in)take of one hundred pupils.

26.  Many doctors have (re / in / inter)jected the government's new plans for the NHS.

27.  Luke missed the (inter / re / im)play of last week's Arsenal and Chelsea match.

28.  The stubborn knight (in / re / inter)fused to take the old woman's advice.

29.  Follow this road until it (inter / in / re)sects with Park Avenue, then turn left.

30.  Once again, we have been (im / re / in)formed that the elevator is not working.

31.  "These rare flowers," said the journalist, "have been (im / re / in)ported from China."

32.  Please (im / re / inter)connect your computer to the Internet and try again.

33.  We were (in / im / re)pelled by the stench of the week-old rubbish.

34.  Mount Tringo, a volcano in the Pacific, has been (im / re / in)active for over fifty years.

35.  This is only an (in / inter / im)mediate solution; we still need to find a permanent one.

36.  You will (in / re / im)cur another fine if you don't return your library books tomorrow.

37.  The local clinic has facilities for those with (in / re / im)paired hearing.

38.  As Peter lies so frequently, I'm not (im / in / re)clined to believe any of his complaints.

Complete the following statements using the prefix <u>im-</u>, <u>in-</u>, <u>re-</u>, or <u>inter-</u>. Then write the correctly spelt word in the space provided.

*<u>Example:</u>* ___ + work ⇨ _____

<u>re</u> + work ⇨ ___rework___

39. _____ + national ⇨ _____
40. _____ + decorate ⇨ _____
41. _____ + prove ⇨ _____
42. _____ + humane ⇨ _____
43. _____ + accurate ⇨ _____
44. _____ + act ⇨ _____
45. _____ + claim ⇨ _____
46. _____ + change ⇨ _____
47. _____ + polite ⇨ _____
48. _____ + acquaint ⇨ _____
49. _____ + formal ⇨ _____
50. _____ + city ⇨ _____
51. _____ + plant ⇨ _____
52. _____ + library ⇨ _____
53. _____ + fund ⇨ _____
54. _____ + consider ⇨ _____

55. _____ + destructible ⇨ _____
56. _____ + personal ⇨ _____
57. _____ + mission ⇨ _____
58. _____ + capable ⇨ _____
59. _____ + dignity ⇨ _____
60. _____ + boot ⇨ _____
61. _____ + mobile ⇨ _____
62. _____ + compatible ⇨ _____
63. _____ + twine ⇨ _____
64. _____ + generate ⇨ _____
65. _____ + separable ⇨ _____
66. _____ + plausible ⇨ _____
67. _____ + material ⇨ _____
68. _____ + galactic ⇨ _____
69. _____ + conclusive ⇨ _____
70. _____ + pertinent ⇨ _____

In each of the following groups, three words end with the same sound. Identify the one word that does NOT sound the same as the others and write it in the space provided.

*Example:* **wait    plait    freight    slate**

wait    plait    freight    slate          _____

_plait_

1.   rough    tough    ruff    cough          _____

2.   doubt    drought    route    clout          _____

3.   foe    tow    dough    vow          _____

4.   trout    bought    wart    fraught          _____

5.   thorough    duller    cower    colour          _____

6.   trough    plough    bough    thou          _____

7.   ewe    true    through    rogue          _____

8.   thought    naught    draught    wrought          _____

9.   hour    flower    borough    sour          _____

10.   nought    caught    quart    chart          _____

11.   south    sought    sort    fort          _____

12.   fought    pout    taut    taught          _____

13.   throughout    nowt    gout    throat          _____

14.   bellow    furlough    sallow    allow          _____

15.   bout    ought    thwart    distraught          _____

16.   although    below    hiccough    woe          _____

---

**Read each sentence carefully. Then complete the statements beneath each sentence. Write your answers in the spaces provided.**

*Example:*   *You must always use knives carefully.*
                *The word with the silent letter is <u>knives</u>. The silent letter is <u>k</u>.*

1.   "I have no doubts at all that everything will work out in the end!" said Janet.
    The word with the silent letter is _____. The silent letter is _____.

2.   On Friday, Poppy slipped on the icy pavement and pulled a muscle in her leg.
    The word with the silent letter is _____. The silent letter is _____.

3.   We aren't sure if the island of Atlantis actually existed or if it is just a myth.
    The word with the silent letter is _____. The silent letter is _____.

4.   Carol always has three digestive biscuits with her cup of coffee in the afternoon.
    The word with the silent letter is _____. The silent letter is _____.

5.   "I think the minted lamb chops with chips is the best dish on the menu," Ash said.
    The word with the silent letter is _____. The silent letter is _____.

6.   As we arrived at the mansion, we noticed that several vehicles were parked outside.
    The word with the silent letter is _____. The silent letter is _____.

7.   "You have no business snooping about in my room," Gina said to her brother angrily.
    The word with the silent letter is _____. The silent letter is _____.

8.   "The time has come," announced the King of the Elves solemnly, "for us to leave Avalon."
    The word with the silent letter is _____. The silent letter is _____.

9.   Harry succumbed to temptation and treated himself to an expensive holiday.
    The word with the silent letter is _____. The silent letter is _____.

10. I have just discovered that the national emblem of Scotland is the thistle.
    The word with the silent letter is _____. The silent letter is _____.

11. We can't stand the cologne that our grandmother uses; it smells positively awful!
    The word with the silent letter is _____. The silent letter is _____.

One word in each of the following sentences is missing a letter string. Read the sentence carefully to work out what the word is. Then, fill in the missing letters so that the word is spelt correctly. Watch out for silent letters!

*Example:* *Every morning, Ashish brushes his teeth and c_____s his hair.*
*Every morning, Ashish brushes his teeth and <u>comb</u>s his hair.*

12.  The young children were f_____d by the colourful fish in the aquarium.

13.  The a_____t discovered the tomb of an ancient Egyptian princess in Thebes.

14.  Bill's dog is a terrible n_____e; it keeps burying bones in my back garden.

15.  People q_____d for over two hours to get into the popular shopping mall.

16.  The Old Man of the Sea's face was very w_____d, but he had kindly eyes.

17.  The police dogs picked up the robber's s_____t very easily.

18.  A w_____k of a treasure ship that sank in the Adriatic has been found.

19.  The word 'chilly' r_____s with the word 'silly'.

20.  "Would you like your r_____t?" the pleasant cashier asked me.

21.  The fox pricked up its ears; something was r_____g in the nearby bushes.

22.  "All c_____s must be handled with great care," said our science teacher.

23.  There are no g_____s that our plan will work, but we must try something!

24.  Realising his prisoners had escaped, the giant g_____d his teeth angrily.

25.  Last year, poor Paolo caught p_____a and was very ill indeed.

26.  As he was in d_____e, nobody recognised the famous film star.

27.  I owe a huge d_____t of gratitude to everyone who has supported me.

28.  The young shepherd put some bread and cheese in his k_____k and set off.

29.  Local residents are c_____g very hard for their library to stay open.

30.  C_____s, like those in Rome, are ancient underground cemeteries.

In each of the following, add as many of the word endings as possible in the Word Endings Bank to each of the given root words, making any necessary changes. Write your answers in the boxes provided. Be careful: some root words will accept more word endings than others.

**_Example:_**

| urge |
|---|
| urgent |
| urgency |

## WORD ENDINGS BANK

-ant     -ance     -ancy     -ent     -ence     -ency

1. observe

2. differ

3. hinder

4. obey

5. hesitate

6. expect

7. reside

8. assist

9. correspond

10. suffice

11. survey

12. depend

# UNIT 16 WORD ENDINGS  -ant, -ance, -ancy, -ent, -ence, & -ency

> **Each of the following sentences contains ONE spelling mistake. Find the misspelt word and write the correct spelling on the line beneath the sentence.**
>
> **_Example:_**  *The soothing fragrence of freshly baked bread filled the air.*
>
> _____fragrance_____

13. There has been a noticeable increment in the efficiency of our staff this year.

   _____

14. That seemingly innocent-looking plant contains a poisonous substence.

   _____

15. I believe in the fundamental decency and tolerence of humanity.

   _____

16. The supporters of the independant candidate were confident she would win the vote.

   _____

17. The frequency of the customer's insistant demands was tiresome.

   _____

18. "Your persistent disobedeience is very disappointing," said the teacher.

   _____

19. I must have your assurances that you will not be negligient in this matter.

   _____

20. The recipiant of this writer's award must possess both eloquence and brilliance.

   _____

21. The defiant endurance and resiliance of the rebel leader were extremely impressive.

   _____

22. A key componant of a coherent, competent piece of writing is good structure.

   _____

23. The malevolent judge showed no leniance in the extended sentences that he passed.

   _____

24. The extent of his inefficiency was apparent to us all, as was his incompetance.

   _____

> **For each of the following, select the word that correctly completes the sentence.**
>
> **_Example:_**   **Sheila always has (one / won) biscuit with her cup of tea.**
> Sheila always has (<u>one</u> / won) biscuit with her cup of tea.

1. There was nothing they could do to (altar / alter) the headmaster's decision.

2. It is usually a good idea to (draught / draft) your ideas before beginning your essay.

3. My grandmother always used to say, "(Practice / Practise) makes perfect."

4. Oedipus correctly (guest / guessed) the answer to the Sphinx's riddle.

5. A day of national (morning / mourning) has been declared.

6. (Steel / Steal) is an alloy that is a mixture of iron and other metals.

7. Do you have any idea (who's / whose) in charge of this department?

8. Julian always (bruise / brews) a pot of peppermint tea for us whenever we visit him.

9. The wounded (heart / hart) was surrounded by the huntsmen's dogs.

10. "I'm afraid I cannot (accept / except) this gift; it's far too expensive," said Pia firmly.

11. The (principle / principal) cause of this problem is a lack of organisation.

12. There is a very good (stationery / stationary) shop on St Peter's Avenue.

13. The brave general (led / lead) his troops into battle.

14. The spoilt child began to (ball / bawl) when its mother took its toys away.

15. The claim that The (Great / Grate) Wall of China can be seen from the moon is untrue.

16. I am always (wary / weary) of things that seem too good to be true.

17. The mad scientist tried to (device / devise) a time-travelling machine.

18. "This TV (cereal / serial) is one of the worst that I've seen in ages!" said the reviewer.

19. The Prime Minister refused to (ascent / assent) to the plan.

20. "I would like to make one (further / farther) suggestion," Micha said.

21. Surprisingly, the (bridal / bridle) party arrived at the church on time.

22. As we have been working hard, I believe we would all (prophet / profit) from a break.

23. The debate has had no (affect / effect) whatsoever on people's views.

24. The (herd / heard) of buffalo moved slowly across the prairie.

25. "What are we having for (desert / dessert)?" asked Phil.

26. The new carpet in the living room (compliments / complements) the sofa nicely.

27. Fresh fruit and vegetables are to be found in the last (aisle / isle).

28. "We must (proceed / precede) quietly so as not to wake the dragon," whispered Sinbad.

29. The school is (lightning / lightening) our classrooms by painting them white.

30. "You should not (meddle / medal) with magic you don't understand," warned Merlin.

31. In some countries, you need a special (license / licence) to own a dog.

32. As the bus went (past / passed), a crowd of tourists waved at us.

33. The following instructions should be read (aloud / allowed) to the students.

34. There was a great deal of (descent / dissent) among the billionaire's heirs.

35. "I (prophecy / prophesy) that you will become king," the strange woman told the knight.

36. As the fog was so dense, Sherlock Holmes (missed / mist) a crucial clue.

37. The forecaster doesn't know (weather / whether) it will rain tomorrow or not.

38. "That is the worst piece of (advice / advise) anyone has given me," snorted Ivy.

39. The (currant / current) economic situation in Europe is very worrying.

40. Being a nurse requires a great deal of (patients / patience).

41. The distraught mother (wrung / rung) her hands in despair.

See how well you remember the correct spellings of the words in Units 13-17! In all of the following tests, show whether each word is correct or incorrect.

*Examples:*    *hello*    ☑
         *wellcome*    ☒

## TEST 18.1

1. allow ☐
2. boute ☐
3. chart ☐
4. device ☐
5. differrent ☐
6. doubt ☐
7. exept ☐
8. flower ☐
9. imaterial ☐
10. impacient ☐
11. imported ☐
12. inactive ☐
13. ineffiecency ☐
14. incorrect ☐
15. international ☐
16. island ☐
17. obediant ☐
18. practice ☐
19. resedency ☐
20. south ☐

SCORE _____ /20

## TEST 18.2

1. assistence ☐
2. although ☐
3. cereial ☐
4. chemicles ☐
5. deppendence ☐
6. disguize ☐
7. duller ☐
8. hesitent ☐
9. immediate ☐
10. inpersonal ☐
11. incapabable ☐
12. in-formal ☐
13. indignity ☐
14. intresects ☐
15. lamb ☐
16. mournning ☐
17. noughty ☐
18. poute ☐
19. rogue ☐
20. seriel ☐

SCORE _____ /20

## TEST 18.3

1. acsent ☐
2. biscuits ☐
3. colour ☐
4. confident ☐
5. descency ☐
6. draught ☐
7. foughted ☐
8. imigrate ☐
9. imbalance ☐
10. implied ☐
11. indefinate ☐
12. inhumain ☐
13. inconclusive ☐
14. interview ☐
15. invallid ☐
16. lienience ☐
17. muscel ☐
18. principel ☐
19. queued ☐
20. stationiery ☐

SCORE _____ /20

## TEST 18.4

1. allowed ☐
2. bought ☐
3. competance ☐
4. discent ☐
5. differance ☐
6. dough ☐
7. grate ☐
8. immoral ☐
9. inpolite ☐
10. inedibble ☐
11. injected ☐
12. incompetence ☐
13. intercity ☐
14. missed ☐
15. nuiscance ☐
16. proceede ☐
17. prophecy ☐
18. reaquaint ☐
19. resident ☐
20. sallow ☐
21. sour ☐
22. thurough ☐

SCORE _____ /22

## TEST 18.5

1. apparrent ☐
2. bellow ☐
3. collogne ☐
4. caughten ☐
5. devise ☐
6. facsinated ☐
7. hinderance ☐
8. immature ☐
9. inpractical ☐
10. infamous ☐
11. innovate ☐
12. lisence ☐
13. medle ☐
14. quart ☐
15. reboot ☐
16. repaired ☐
17. refund ☐
18. retake ☐
19. scent ☐
20. taught ☐
21. wether ☐
22. wrinckled ☐

SCORE _____ /22

## TEST 18.6

1. advice ☐
2. accept ☐
3. curant ☐
4. cower ☐
5. dett ☐
6. expectance ☐
7. hicough ☐
8. improve ☐
9. inmobile ☐
10. injustice ☐
11. inseparible ☐
12. interlibary ☐
13. lightning ☐
14. naught ☐
15. persistant ☐
16. reclaim ☐
17. review ☐
18. replay ☐
19. rung ☐
20. sufficient ☐
21. solemly ☐
22. rought ☐

SCORE _____ /22

## TEST 18.7

1. assistent ☐
2. brews ☐
3. complaments ☐
4. cought ☐
5. dependancy ☐
6. gnashed ☐
7. impairred ☐
8. innocent ☐
9. inacurrate ☐
10. incremente ☐
11. observence ☐
12. profit ☐
13. patience ☐
14. redecorate ☐
15. reconnect ☐
16. rhyhms ☐
17. stationary ☐
18. saught ☐
19. thissle ☐
20. thoughted ☐
21. wart ☐
22. woe ☐

SCORE _____ /22

## TEST 18.8

1. alltar ☐
2. component ☐
3. clout ☐
4. deffiant ☐
5. endurancy ☐
6. frought ☐
7. frequency ☐
8. impelled ☐
9. insuffiscient ☐
10. inadvisable ☐
11. intermission ☐
12. negligient ☐
13. reformed ☐
14. redirect ☐
15. recepit ☐
16. rustleing ☐
17. substants ☐
18. through ☐
19. trout ☐
20. weary ☐
21. wrek ☐
22. vehicels ☐

SCORE _____ /22

## TEST 18.9

1. assent ☐
2. below ☐
3. correspondant ☐
4. doubts ☐
5. futher ☐
6. implant ☐
7. intake ☐
8. inclined ☐
9. intertwine ☐
10. malevolant ☐
11. ought ☐
12. obedience ☐
13. prophesy ☐
14. reggenerate ☐
15. refused ☐
16. reconsider ☐
17. rough ☐
18. throut ☐
19. tough ☐
20. tolerence ☐
21. wheather ☐
22. wrung ☐

SCORE _____ /22

## TEST 18.10

1. advise ☐
2. archeologist ☐
3. bawl ☐
4. compliament ☐
5. coherant ☐
6. dessent ☐
7. disobedience ☐
8. efficience ☐
9. farther ☐
10. gout ☐
11. hesitance ☐
12. immortal ☐
13. inpertinent ☐
14. inadecquate ☐
15. independent ☐
16. intermediate ☐
17. lisense ☐
18. prinsiple ☐
19. residence ☐
20. reported ☐
21. sufficiancy ☐
22. through-out ☐

SCORE _____ /22

## TEST 18.11

1. alloud ☐
2. bridel ☐
3. business ☐
4. current ☐
5. catacoombs ☐
6. dependent ☐
7. drought ☐
8. expectent ☐
9. foe ☐
10. immovible ☐
11. imprescise ☐
12. incompatible ☐
13. informed ☐
14. intergalactic ☐
15. meddel ☐
16. observent ☐
17. preceede ☐
18. prophit ☐
19. repelled ☐
20. recurr ☐
21. surveillence ☐
22. taut ☐

SCORE _____ /22

## TEST 18.12

1. assurrances ☐
2. burrough ☐
3. correspondance ☐
4. campaining ☐
5. distraught ☐
6. eloquents ☐
7. furrlough ☐
8. guarantees ☐
9. implausable ☐
10. inprudent ☐
11. indestructable ☐
12. inattentive ☐
13. interjected ☐
14. napsack ☐
15. lightenning ☐
16. patients ☐
17. pnuemonia ☐
18. resillience ☐
19. recipiant ☐
20. route ☐
21. sucumbed ☐
22. thwart ☐

SCORE _____ /22

> **For each of the following, select the one prefix from the choices given that correctly completes the given word.**
>
> _Example:_  "The phone that you sold me yesterday is ___standard," complained Mr Brown.
> - [ ] super
> - [ ] anti
> - [x] sub
> - [ ] sub-

1. All of these items can be bought at your local ___market.
   - [ ] anti
   - [ ] sub
   - [ ] auto
   - [ ] super

2. The local council is forming a special ___committee to investigate this matter.
   - [ ] sub-
   - [ ] sub
   - [ ] super
   - [ ] super-

3. "You need to put some ___septic on that wound," the nurse told Emma.
   - [ ] auto
   - [ ] super
   - [ ] sub
   - [ ] anti

4. Scientists have divided the animal kingdom into numerous ___categories.
   - [ ] sub
   - [ ] auto-
   - [ ] anti-
   - [ ] super

5. The teenage fans went wild when their favourite ___stars emerged from their limos.
   - [ ] auto
   - [ ] anti
   - [ ] super
   - [ ] sub

6. I would love to own an ___graph of a famous novelist.
   - [ ] super
   - [ ] auto
   - [ ] sub
   - [ ] anti

7. Lola's memories of her childhood were buried deep in her ___conscious.
   - [ ] anti
   - [ ] auto
   - [ ] super
   - [ ] sub

8. After all the excitement of the holidays, going back to work was an ___climax.
   - [ ] sub-
   - [ ] super-
   - [ ] anti-
   - [ ] anti

9. The HMS Seahorse was a ___marine that was sunk during World War II.
   - [ ] super
   - [ ] anti
   - [ ] sub
   - [ ] auto-

10. Sophie enjoys reading ___biographies of famous actors.
    - [ ] auto
    - [ ] auto-
    - [ ] super
    - [ ] anti-

> In each of the following, use an appropriate prefix from the Prefix Bank with the root word supplied in brackets to create a correctly spelt new word that sensibly completes each sentence. Remember to use hyphens where necessary.
>
> _**Example:**_ ***Many heroes in myths from around the world possess _____. (powers)***
> _Many heroes in myths from around the world possess underlined{superpowers}. (powers)_

### PREFIX BANK

sub-        super-        anti-        auto-

11. To switch the oven off, you must turn this knob _____. (clockwise)

12. The wyvern is a _____ creature that is part dragon, part griffin. (natural)

13. "Remember to give your article a _____," our teacher reminded us. (title)

14. According to ancient Greek myths, Hercules, had _____ strength. (human)

15. What do you get if you _____ 634 from 1,597? (tract)

16. Mr Howard has had his car fitted with an _____device. (theft)

17. Tom believes he's a _____; he's always trying to do the impossible. (man)

18. The town was almost completely _____ by the flood. (merged)

19. In the past, people used to call cars _____. (mobiles)

20. I think I can fix that broken vase with some _____. (glue)

21. An _____ is a type of medicine used to treat certain diseases. (biotic)

22. The photographer has _____ an image over the original one. (imposed)

23. The teacher _____ the class into three teams of ten. (divided)

24. _____ is the North American word for an underground railway. (way)

25. The _____ of the thriller was 'Be Very Afraid!'. (heading)

26. Every year, _____ become faster and faster. (computers)

27. Hilda works as a _____ at our local newspaper. (editor)

Complete the following tables with the correctly spelt plural form of each given word.

| Example: | Singular | Plural |
|---|---|---|
| | dog | dogs |

| SINGULAR | PLURAL |
|---|---|
| 1.  girl | |
| 2.  knave | |
| 3.  tomato | |
| 4.  celebration | |
| 5.  woman | |
| 6.  mouse | |
| 7.  ibis | |
| 8.  anniversary | |
| 9.  foot | |
| 10. man | |
| 11. sheep | |
| 12. privilege | |
| 13. rhythm | |
| 14. ox | |
| 15. igloo | |
| 16. child | |
| 17. tooth | |

| SINGULAR | PLURAL |
|---|---|
| 18. goose | |
| 19. distillery | |
| 20. attendee | |
| 21. fox | |
| 22. this | |
| 23. miniature | |
| 24. wife | |
| 25. cactus | |
| 26. liability | |
| 27. louse | |
| 28. volcano | |
| 29. allegory | |
| 30. loaf | |
| 31. crisis | |
| 32. deer | |
| 33. that | |
| 34. phenomenon | |

> **For each of the following, underline the one correct spelling from the choices given in brackets.**
>
> **_Example:_** **The (flower's  flowers  flowers'  flowers's) bobbed gently in the summer breeze.**
>
> The (flower's  <u>flowers</u>  flowers'  flowers's) bobbed gently in the summer breeze.

35. The (childrens  childrens'  children's  childrenes) laughter filled the air.

36. Many of the (soldierses'  soldiers  soldiers's  soldiers') wounds never healed properly.

37. The (fish's  fishes  fishes'  fishes's) were all covered with fluorescent scales.

38. Miriam has broken her father's (glasses  glassess  glasses's  glasses') again.

39. Tara's new (shoes  shoe's  shoeses  shoes') heels are extremely thin and high.

40. We will always have (controversies'  controversys  controversies  controversie's).

41. The fans threw their (scarve's  scarves  scarves'  scarves's) into the air in celebration.

42. The (amateures'  amateures  amateurs's  amateurs') drama club is held on Mondays.

43. The (firemen  firemans'  firemen's  firemens's) bravery was astonishing.

44. My favourite biscuits are triple chocolate-chip (cookies  cookys  cooky's  cookieses).

45. This device can't pick up those (radio's  radioes  radioes'  radios') signals.

46. The (Peopleses  Peoples'  People's  Peopleses') Republic of China is in Asia.

47. The White (Cliff's  Cliffes  Cliffes's  Cliffs) of Dover are a world-famous landmark.

48. Various kinds of mushrooms are (funguses'  fungis  fungi  fungus's) that are edible.

49. Sherine dislikes both (avocados  avocadoes's  avocadoes'  avocados') and guavas.

50. Turn to the back of the book for all the (quizzes  quizes  quizz's  quizzes') solutions.

51. Various deserts all over the world possess stunning (oasis'  oasises  oases  oaseses).

52. The (puppies  puppys  puppy's  puppies') tails wagged excitedly when Gill came in.

53. There has been a (series  serie  serie's  serieses) of complaints made.

54. The ancient Egyptians greatly feared (hippopotamii  hippopotamuses  hippopotamis  hippopotamuses').

---

> For each of the following, add an appropriate suffix to the root word supplied in brackets to complete the sentence in the most sensible way. Write the correctly spelt word in the space provided.
>
> **_Example:_**  **_"Paul is doing really well!" said his sister excitedly. "It looks as though he is _____!" (win)_**
>
> _"Paul is doing really well!" said his sister excitedly. "It looks as though he is <u>winning</u>!" (win)_

1. Although Tom is just a _____, he is learning very quickly. (begin)

2. The estate employs a _____ to look after the grounds. (garden)

3. Our history teacher is an excellent _____. (communicate)

4. I have _____ all the chemistry I learned at school. (forget)

5. They have placed a _____ on imports from Russia. (limit)

6. That car is _____ with a TomTom sat nav. (equip)

7. When I was little, I got very badly _____ one summer. (sunburn)

8. The billionaire owned a highly successful _____ company. (ship)

9. We have no idea why this glitch keeps _____. (occur)

10. My parents keep _____ me to study harder. (nag)

11. All the _____ for the school fair have been completed. (prepare)

12. The accused was _____ by the court. (acquit)

13. My father is a very talented chemical _____. (engine)

14. Penny spent ages _____ with the shopkeeper. (bargain)

15. Many areas in the country suffer from _____. (overpopulate)

16. The last _____ we had was called Marnie. (babysit)

17. Keith has _____ all the responsibility for this. (shoulder)

18. Neil sat in the corner and gently _____ his guitar. (strum)

19. An aircraft _____ is a warship from which planes take off. (carry)

> For each of the following, select the one letter string that correctly completes the given word. Each word has been defined to help you.
>
> *Example:* P_____T (adj.): nice
> A. LESAN     (B.) LEASAN     C. LEASSAN     D. LEASEN

20. A_____D (v.): gave a person a place to stay
    A. COMODATE    B. COMMADATE    C. CCOMMODATE    D. CCOMMADATTE

21. I_____G (v.): taking steps to try to prevent something bad from happening
    A. NSURIN    B. NSURRIN    C. NSSURIN    D. NSSURRIN

22. F_____D (v.): shaped or designed something a particular way
    A. ORMATE    B. ORMMATTE    C. ORMMATE    D. ORMATTE

23. E_____G (v.): giving out (sound, light, etc.)
    A. MITIN    B. MMITIN    C. MITTIN    D. MMITTIN

24. U_____D (v.): lacked concentration or attention
    A. NFFOCUSE    B. NFOCUSE    C. NFOCCUSSE    D. NFOCCUSE

25. E_____T (n.): a feeling of self-conscious awkwardness
    A. MMBARASMEN    B. MBARASMEN    C. MBARASSMEN    D. MBARRASSMEN

26. D_____T (n.): a result or consequence
    A. EVELOPPMEN    B. EVELOPMEN    C. EVELLOPMEN    D. EVALOPMEN

27. E_____R (n.): a person who listens secretly to a private conversation
    A. VESDROPPE    B. VESDROPE    C. AVESDDROPE    D. AVESDROPPE

28. P_____D (v.): said or uttered words
    A. RONOUNCE    B. RONNOUNCE    C. RONOUNNCE    D. RONUNCE

29. E_____D (v.): described something as better than it really was
    A. XAGERATE    B. XAGERRATE    C. XAGGERATE    D. XAGGARATE

In each of the following groups, THREE of the four words have been MISSPELT. Complete the statements in the boxes to show which ONE word is CORRECTLY spelt and how the THREE remaining words SHOULD be spelt.

*Example:*  *tabel, chair, carppet, miror*

| |
|---|
| ***The one word that is spelt correctly is*** chair. |

| |
|---|
| ***The three remaining words should be spelt*** table, carpet, mirror. |

1. conferrence, deferral, diffrence, sufferred

| |
|---|
| The one word that is spelt correctly is |

| |
|---|
| The three remaining words should be spelt |

2. offered, infered, surffing, referance

| |
|---|
| The one word that is spelt correctly is |

| |
|---|
| The three remaining words should be spelt |

3. referal, preference, differring, confered

| |
|---|
| The one word that is spelt correctly is |

| |
|---|
| The three remaining words should be spelt |

4. referrendum, transferance, pilferring, refereed

| |
|---|
| The one word that is spelt correctly is |

| |
|---|
| The three remaining words should be spelt |

In each of the following, you are given the definition of a word. Select the one correct spelling of the word that is being defined from the choices given.

*Example:*  *Choice*

   A.   *opcion*          B.   *opption*          C.   *opsion*          (D.)   *option*

5.   A willingness to respect the wishes of other people
     A.   defferrence          B.   deference          C.   deferrence          D.   defference

6.   Discussing or consulting together
     A.   conferring          B.   confering          C.   conffering          D.   confferring

7.   Put something off until a later time
     A.   defered          B.   deffered          C.   deferred          D.   defferred

8.   Stating one's willingness to do something
     A.   ofering          B.   offerring          C.   oferring          D.   offering

9.   A judgement or conclusion based on facts
     A.   inference          B.   inferrence          C.   infferrence          D.   infference

10.  Stole
     A.   pilffered          B.   pilfered          C.   pilferred          D.   pilfferred

11.  Distress or pain
     A.   sufferring          B.   suferring          C.   suffering          D.   sufering

12.  A person who stands or lies on a narrow board and tries to ride waves to the shore
     A.   surfer          B.   surrfer          C.   surffer          D.   surferer

13.  Liked one thing more than another
     A.   prefferred          B.   preffered          C.   prefered          D.   preferred

14.  To meddle in something that is not one's business
     A.   interferre          B.   interfere          C.   interfferre          D.   interffere

Add the word ending <u>-tion</u>, <u>-sion</u>, <u>-ssion</u>, or <u>-cian</u> to each given root word to complete every statement. Make any necessary changes, then write the correctly spelt word in the space provided.

*Example:*  *delete +* ___ ⇨ _____

         *delete + <u>tion</u>* ⇨ _____*deletion*_____

1.  music + _____ ⇨ _____

2.  commit + _____ ⇨ _____

3.  decide + _____ ⇨ _____

4.  educate + _____ ⇨ _____

5.  discuss + _____ ⇨ _____

6.  adopt + _____ ⇨ _____

7.  include + _____ ⇨ _____

8.  operate + _____ ⇨ _____

9.  suggest + _____ ⇨ _____

10. electric + _____ ⇨ _____

11. predict + _____ ⇨ _____

12. express + _____ ⇨ _____

13. submit + _____ ⇨ _____

14. elect + _____ ⇨ _____

15. promote + _____ ⇨ _____

16. divide + _____ ⇨ _____

17. comprehend + _____ ⇨ _____

18. attend + _____ ⇨ _____

19. compress + _____ ⇨ _____

20. insert + _____ ⇨ _____

21. diffuse + _____ ⇨ _____

22. omit + _____ ⇨ _____

23. distort + _____ ⇨ _____

24. suspend + _____ ⇨ _____

25. profess + _____ ⇨ _____

26. graduate + _____ ⇨ _____

27. project + _____ ⇨ _____

28. devote + _____ ⇨ _____

29. contract + _____ ⇨ _____

30. clinic + _____ ⇨ _____

31. prevent + _____ ⇨ _____

32. transmit + _____ ⇨ _____

> In each of the following, add the word ending <u>-tion</u>, <u>-sion</u>, <u>-ssion</u>, or <u>-cian</u> to each root word given in brackets. Make any necessary changes, then use the correctly spelt word to complete the sentence.
>
> *Example:* _____ *films now cost huge sums of money. (act)*
>     <u>Action</u> *films now cost huge sums of money. (act)*

33.  Please submit an _____ with your project. (illustrate)

34.  Ali wants to become an _____ when he grows up. (optic)

35.  I think we made a good _____ at the meeting. (impress)

36.  Levels of _____ have reached a record high. (pollute)

37.  The criminal refused to make an _____ of guilt. (admit)

38.  The new curriculum has caused much _____. (confuse)

39.  I have a _____ to make; I've broken your TV. (confess)

40.  Sally gave no _____ that anything was wrong. (indicate)

41.  Mrs Tully was prepared to make an _____ for us. (except)

42.  The teacher has given us _____ to leave early. (permit)

43.  Ian collapsed on the sofa in utter _____. (exhaust)

44.  There has been a large _____ at a shoe factory. (explode)

45.  A _____ needs to be very good with numbers. (statistic)

46.  "My _____ is utterly honourable," swore Ed. (intend)

47.  The hotel offers _____ for large families. (accommodate)

48.  The stomach is responsible for food _____. (digest)

49.  "I apologise for the _____," said Mabel. (intrude)

50.  The cowardly soldier was found guilty of _____. (desert)

51.  The _____ of greenhouse gases must be curbed. (emit)

See how well you remember the correct spellings of the words in Units 19-23! In all of the following tests, show whether each word is correct or incorrect.

_Examples:_      hello          ☑

                  wellcome     ☒

## TEST 24.1

1. adoption ☐
2. anticlockwise ☐
3. babysit ☐
4. cactus ☐
5. cactuses ☐
6. catagories ☐
7. child ☐
8. commitee ☐
9. differrence ☐
10. engine ☐
11. education ☐
12. fox ☐
13. garden ☐
14. iggloo ☐
15. loaves ☐
16. musician ☐
17. ocurr ☐
18. preperations ☐
19. quizzes' ☐
20. rythms ☐

SCORE _____ /20

## TEST 24.2

1. autobiographes ☐
2. bargain ☐
3. carrier ☐
4. celebration ☐
5. conferrence ☐
6. deer ☐
7. divided ☐
8. desert ☐
9. descision ☐
10. forget ☐
11. fishes's ☐
12. girl ☐
13. gooses ☐
14. liability ☐
15. merged ☐
16. oxe ☐
17. privilige ☐
18. peoples's ☐
19. refferral ☐
20. sufferring ☐

SCORE _____ /20

## TEST 24.3

1. aquitt ☐
2. allegry ☐
3. antitheft ☐
4. begin ☐
5. communnicate ☐
6. contractian ☐
7. defered ☐
8. distillary ☐
9. developpment ☐
10. electian ☐
11. foot ☐
12. glasseses ☐
13. impose ☐
14. knave ☐
15. limitation ☐
16. man ☐
17. pilfererd ☐
18. phenomemon ☐
19. sunburnned ☐
20. surfing ☐

SCORE _____ /20

## TEST 24.4

1.   accommadated ☐
2.   antibiotic ☐
3.   confussion ☐
4.   cookies ☐
5.   digestion ☐
6.   discusssion ☐
7.   equip ☐
8.   electrician ☐
9.   geeses ☐
10.  illlustration ☐
11.  ibis ☐
12.  insertion ☐
13.  minature ☐
14.  offerred ☐
15.  pollutian ☐
16.  proffession ☐
17.  shoulder ☐
18.  suspention ☐
19.  suggestian ☐
20.  subway ☐
21.  superman ☐
22.  tomatoe ☐

SCORE _____ /22

## TEST 24.5

1.   aniversaries ☐
2.   attendee ☐
3.   confered ☐
4.   childrens's ☐
5.   commission ☐
6.   deferance ☐
7.   explosion ☐
8.   girls ☐
9.   iglooes ☐
10.  men ☐
11.  overpoppulate ☐
12.  ommission ☐
13.  prediction ☐
14.  preferrence ☐
15.  prefferred ☐
16.  referrence ☐
17.  refereed ☐
18.  strum ☐
19.  shiping ☐
20.  subdivided ☐
21.  subtract ☐
22.  teeth ☐

SCORE _____ /22

## TEST 24.6

1.   attention ☐
2.   childs' ☐
3.   celebrations ☐
4.   crisses ☐
5.   deers ☐
6.   division ☐
7.   impression ☐
8.   interferre ☐
9.   limit ☐
10.  nag ☐
11.  projection ☐
12.  pro-nounced ☐
13.  soldier's ☐
14.  serie's ☐
15.  shoe's ☐
16.  surfer ☐
17.  sunburnt ☐
18.  subcommitee ☐
19.  subtitle ☐
20.  superglue ☐
21.  this ☐
22.  unfoccused ☐

SCORE _____ /22

## TEST 24.7

1. autograph ☐
2. bruise ☐
3. carry ☐
4. clockwise ☐
5. distortian ☐
6. expresion ☐
7. gardner ☐
8. knaves ☐
9. occurring ☐
10. operacion ☐
11. prepare ☐
12. prommotion ☐
13. radios' ☐
14. ship ☐
15. subcontious ☐
16. subcatagories ☐
17. superhuman ☐
18. septical ☐
19. statistic ☐
20. volcano ☐
21. whose's ☐
22. wife ☐

SCORE _____ /22

## TEST 24.8

1. amatueurs ☐
2. begginner ☐
3. cliffes ☐
4. comprescion ☐
5. distileries ☐
6. exaggerrated ☐
7. indication ☐
8. inclusion ☐
9. lice ☐
10. mouse ☐
11. prevension ☐
12. sheep ☐
13. submission ☐
14. subheading ☐
15. subediter ☐
16. supermarket ☐
17. tooth ☐
18. these ☐
19. theif ☐
20. that ☐
21. trans-mission ☐
22. woman ☐

SCORE _____ /22

## TEST 24.9

1. admission ☐
2. anticlimax ☐
3. communicater ☐
4. controvesies ☐
5. differring ☐
6. devotion ☐
7. emmitting ☐
8. engineer ☐
9. foxes ☐
10. feets ☐
11. graduation ☐
12. infered ☐
13. oasis ☐
14. permission ☐
15. privileges ☐
16. puppies's ☐
17. referendem ☐
18. sufferred ☐
19. submarine ☐
20. submerged ☐
21. superstars ☐
22. scarves ☐

SCORE _____ /22

## TEST 24.10

1. allegaries ☐
2. anniversary ☐
3. avocadoes ☐
4. babysitter ☐
5. biographies ☐
6. crissis ☐
7. clinician ☐
8. defferral ☐
9. exceptian ☐
10. forggotten ☐
11. intrusion ☐
12. ibeses ☐
13. insuring ☐
14. loaf ☐
15. offerring ☐
16. optiscian ☐
17. oxen ☐
18. pilffering ☐
19. strumed ☐
20. supernatural ☐
21. those ☐
22. who's ☐

SCORE _____ /22

## TEST 24.11

1. attendees ☐
2. automobiles ☐
3. bargainning ☐
4. confession ☐
5. children's ☐
6. dessertion ☐
7. exhuaustion ☐
8. equipped ☐
9. firemens' ☐
10. fungi ☐
11. intention ☐
12. liabilaties ☐
13. mice ☐
14. nagging ☐
15. oasses ☐
16. rhythem ☐
17. shouldered ☐
18. sheeps ☐
19. sunburn ☐
20. supercomputers ☐
21. tomatos ☐
22. volcanos ☐

SCORE _____ /22

## TEST 24.12

1. accommodation ☐
2. acquited ☐
3. antisceptic ☐
4. confering ☐
5. comprehension ☐
6. difussion ☐
7. emission ☐
8. eaveasdropper ☐
9. embarrassment ☐
10. formated ☐
11. hippopotamuses ☐
12. inferrance ☐
13. louse ☐
14. miniatures ☐
15. overpopulation ☐
16. phenomena ☐
17. statistitician ☐
18. superimposed ☐
19. swott ☐
20. transferance ☐
21. women ☐
22. wives's ☐

SCORE _____ /22

In each of the following groups, two out of the five words do not begin with a prefix. Identify the two words that DO NOT START WITH A PREFIX.

*Example:* _____ *misjudge*

_____ *extract*

__X__ *misery*

_____ *enable*

__X__ *ready*

1. _____ supervision
   _____ interested
   _____ disarm
   _____ inaudible
   _____ superb

2. _____ antic
   _____ miscalculate
   _____ ill-advised
   _____ comet
   _____ expose

3. _____ contract
   _____ profess
   _____ discos
   _____ preen
   _____ extraordinary

4. _____ counter
   _____ unabridged
   _____ relative
   _____ reapplied
   _____ misfire

5. _____ increase
   _____ inner
   _____ ungrammatical
   _____ prologue
   _____ mister

6. _____ rebuilt
   _____ comma
   _____ discolour
   _____ coining
   _____ exclude

7. _____ pronoun
   _____ extraterrestrial
   _____ proudly
   _____ reedy
   _____ intervene

8. _____ imagine
   _____ autonomous
   _____ extract
   _____ dishonour
   _____ prowler

9. _____ unrepentant
   _____ antique
   _____ indistinct
   _____ unit
   _____ misplaced

10. _____ comely
    _____ convert
    _____ redeliver
    _____ condor
    _____ disown

11. _____ unresolvable
    _____ inequality
    _____ under
    _____ profiterole
    _____ proactive

12. _____ interred
    _____ disqualify
    _____ refill
    _____ exclaim
    _____ prodigy

13. _____ subcontinent
    _____ mistletoe
    _____ misremembered
    _____ external
    _____ interim

14. _____ inhibit
    _____ supersede
    _____ intern
    _____ properly
    _____ dissatisfied

15. _____ conical
    _____ insignificance
    _____ misdial
    _____ probing
    _____ extracurricular

Complete the following sentences by adding <u>im-</u>, <u>in-</u>, <u>ir-</u>, <u>dis-</u>, or <u>un-</u> to each of the given words to form a word that has the OPPOSITE meaning to the given word.

<u>Example:</u>   **The opposite of perfect is** _____.
      *The opposite of perfect is* <u>imperfect</u>.

16.   The opposite of **perceptible** is _____.

17.   The opposite of **professional** is _____.

18.   The opposite of **accessible** is _____.

19.   The opposite of **advantage** is _____.

20.   The opposite of **compromising** is _____.

21.   The opposite of **considerate** is _____.

22.   The opposite of **characteristic** is _____.

23.   The opposite of **replaceable** is _____.

24.   The opposite of **belief** is _____.

25.   The opposite of **bearable** is _____.

26.   The opposite of **insured** is _____.

27.   The opposite of **animate** is _____.

28.   The opposite of **eligible** is _____.

29.   The opposite of **reconcilable** is _____.

30.   The opposite of **regarded** is _____.

31.   The opposite of **patriotic** is _____.

32.   The opposite of **appropriate** is _____.

33.   The opposite of **remarkable** is _____.

34.   The opposite of **effective** is _____.

# MIXED WORD ENDINGS & SUFFIXES

> 25 words are listed below. However, 10 of them are spelt incorrectly. Find the 10 incorrectly spelt words and write their correct spellings in the spaces provided.

| | | | | |
|---|---|---|---|---|
| uninterested | discontinued | disturbence | inacknowledged | improper |
| improbibly | irredeemable | interlaced | unfashionable | unrelevance |
| imprisonment | reallocated | subdivision | disdiagnose | misapprovingly |
| indrinkable | reevaluation | unadmissible | redoubling | unadvertised |
| subscript | uninvited | automatic | inpersonated | disoriented |

1. _____

2. _____

3. _____

4. _____

5. _____

6. _____

7. _____

8. _____

9. _____

10. _____

> ALL of the following words have been misspelt in at least one way. Write the correct spelling of each word in the space provided.

11. irepairable _____

12. undefinible _____

13. inexperiency _____

14. incouragment _____

15. proficience _____

16. irreverant _____

17. misgoverment _____

18. disaggrment _____

19. unconsistence _____

20. misrespectfull _____

21. reassurence _____

22. imprudance _____

23. inemploymence _____

24. irretreivible _____

Complete the following statements with the correctly spelt root words and appropriate word endings or suffixes.

*Example:* _____ + ___ ⇨ *boyish*

*boy* + *ish* ⇨ *boyish*

25. _____ + _____ ⇨ jabbed

26. _____ + _____ ⇨ presidential

27. _____ + _____ ⇨ inducible

28. _____ + _____ ⇨ guidance

29. _____ + _____ ⇨ differed

30. _____ + _____ ⇨ irritation

31. _____ + _____ ⇨ urgency

32. _____ + _____ ⇨ obsession

33. _____ + _____ ⇨ chiselling

34. _____ + _____ ⇨ compliant

35. _____ + _____ ⇨ invention

36. _____ + _____ ⇨ hysterically

37. _____ + _____ ⇨ persuasion

38. _____ + _____ ⇨ rhetorician

39. _____ + _____ ⇨ ably

40. _____ + _____ ⇨ plodder

41. _____ + _____ ⇨ transferring

42. _____ + _____ ⇨ erosion

43. _____ + _____ ⇨ eerily

44. _____ + _____ ⇨ trekked

45. _____ + _____ ⇨ classifiable

46. _____ + _____ ⇨ idealistically

47. _____ + _____ ⇨ conscientious

48. _____ + _____ ⇨ transgression

49. _____ + _____ ⇨ absorbent

50. _____ + _____ ⇨ forensically

51. _____ + _____ ⇨ consequential

52. _____ + _____ ⇨ occupancy

53. _____ + _____ ⇨ coherence

54. _____ + _____ ⇨ flogging

55. _____ + _____ ⇨ completion

56. _____ + _____ ⇨ succession

Complete the following table with the correctly spelt singular or plural form of each given word.

| Examples: | Singular | Plural |
|---|---|---|
| | cat | cats |
| | book | books |

| SINGULAR | PLURAL | SINGULAR | PLURAL |
|---|---|---|---|
| 1.   mine | | 17.  giraffe | |
| 2. | bosses | 18.  moose | |
| 3. | thieves | 19. | barracks |
| 4.   chief | | 20. | lampshades |
| 5. | complexes | 21. | matchsticks |
| 6.   echo | | 22.  commando | |
| 7. | bookworms | 23. | indices |
| 8.   his | | 24.  belief | |
| 9. | anchovies | 25. | allies |
| 10.  alley | | 26.  torpedo | |
| 11. | mattresses | 27. | yours |
| 12.  puff | | 28.  confectionery | |
| 13.  rhinoceros | | 29.  offspring | |
| 14. | ourselves | 30. | axes |
| 15.  handkerchief | | 31.  zero | |
| 16.  advice | | 32.  archipelago | |

> **Each of the following sentences contains ONE spelling mistake. Find the misspelt word and write the correct spelling on the line beneath the sentence.**
>
> _**Example:**_  _Those girls and boys' are in my class._
>
> _boys_

33.  At the zoo, we saw many animals including snakes, bisons, lions, tigers, and llamas.

     _____

34.  The book contained lots of pictures and interesting informations about the planets.

     _____

35.  The French and Italian ships' cargoes' of luxuries were unloaded at the docks.

     _____

36.  The roof's of the cottages were covered with pretty red tiles that were sixty years old.

     _____

37.  Ulalia gazed up at the beautiful spines lining the bookshelfs in the house's main hall.

     _____

38.  The sound of the oboes's crescendos made the hairs on the back of my neck stand up.

     _____

39.  The young apprentice over-boiled the chef's carrots, potatos, radishes, and leeks.

     _____

40.  Susie loves the rhythms of tangos and calypsos, but she doesn't like those of waltzes'.

     _____

41.  Flames and billowing smoke came out of the two dragons's large nostrils and mouths.

     _____

42.  Mosquitos bites are usually harmless; sometimes, however, they can be dangerous.

     _____

43.  Those dirty shoes over there are yours', as are the dirty clothes on the chairs.

     _____

44.  The gnomes were responsible for the hoax's played on the fairies' children.

     _____

Use the clues given to help you work out what each gender word is. Then, fill in the missing letters of each word so that it is spelt correctly.

*Example:*  **The word for a female horse is  m _ _ _.**
          *The word for a female horse is  m  a  r  e.*

1.  The word for a male duck is **d** ___ ___ ___ ___.

2.  The word for a female duck is **d** ___ ___ ___.

3.  The word for a male chicken is **r** ___ ___ ___ ___ ___ ___.

4.  The word for a female chicken is **h** ___ ___.

5.  The word for a male goose is **g** ___ ___ ___ ___ ___.

6.  The word for a female goose is **g** ___ ___ ___ ___.

7.  The word for a male pig is **b** ___ ___ ___.

8.  The word for a female pig is **s** ___ ___.

9.  The word for a male sheep is **r** ___ ___.

10. The word for a female sheep is **e** ___ ___.

11. The word for a male cat is **t** ___ ___.

12. The word for a female tiger is **t** ___ ___ ___ ___ ___ ___.

13. The word for a male bee is **d** ___ ___ ___ ___.

14. The word for a male deer is **s** ___ ___ ___.

15. The word for a female fox is **v** ___ ___ ___ ___.

16. The word for a female peacock is **p** ___ ___ ___ ___ ___.

17. The word for a male whale is **b** ___ ___ ___.

18. The word for a female whale is **c** ___ ___.

Complete the following tables with the correctly spelt missing gender form of each given word.

**Examples:**

| MASCULINE | FEMININE |
| --- | --- |
| man | woman |
| king | queen |

| MASCULINE | FEMININE |
| --- | --- |
| 19. duke | |
| 20. | bride |
| 21. heir | |
| 22. | lady |
| 23. | shepherdess |
| 24. son | |
| 25. | waitress |
| 26. brother | |
| 27. abbot | |
| 28. manservant | |
| 29. | heroine |
| 30. steward | |
| 31. Mr | |
| 32. lad | |
| 33. | princess |
| 34. | mistress |

| MASCULINE | FEMININE |
| --- | --- |
| 35. earl | |
| 36. headmaster | |
| 37. god | |
| 38. emperor | |
| 39. | madam |
| 40. actor | |
| 41. | dam |
| 42. sultan | |
| 43. | witch |
| 44. | widow |
| 45. monk | |
| 46. bachelor | |
| 47. uncle | |
| 48. marquis | |
| 49. | fiancée |
| 50. | nanny goat |

> **For each of the following, select the word that correctly completes the sentence.**
>
> *Example:*   **Sheila always has (one / won) biscuit with her cup of tea.**
>      *Sheila always has (<u>one</u> / won) biscuit with her cup of tea.*

1. Pablo and Gamal made a (pact / packed) to remain best friends, no matter what.

2. "I believe that finding a cure for this disease is (eminent / imminent)," said Dr Polly.

3. "Over there," said Ivy, pointing at a bench. "That's where (were / we're) sitting."

4. None of the men in the town responded to the Sheriff's call to (alms / arms).

5. At the (bazaar / bizarre), we found many strange and wonderful spices, silks, and trinkets.

6. "This quest will test the (metal / mettle) of all my knights," announced King Arthur.

7. For my (aural / oral) test tomorrow, I have to recite a sonnet by Shakespeare.

8. The author wrote an interesting (foreword / forward) for her new book.

9. You will need three (quartz / quarts) of milk for this recipe.

10. "Such suspense simply cannot be (born / borne)! I must know the answer!" wailed Di.

11. If those children are left unattended, they will (reek / wreak) havoc.

12. Jehan is a real (swot / swat); she studies all the time, even at weekends!

13. The flour in the packet that we bought was surprisingly (course / coarse).

14. The (troop / troupe) of monkeys we saw at the circus performed some amazing tricks.

15. One way to kill a vampire is to drive a wooden (steak / stake) through its heart.

16. Mr Deloney and Mr Swift will fight a (duel / dual) with pistols at dawn tomorrow.

17. The government has (sort / sought) to find a solution to this problem, but has failed.

18. The Americans and the Japanese fought several (naval / navel) battles in World War II.

19. The poor frog was (cast / caste) aside by the unfeeling princess.

20. Jeanette couldn't decide (wear / where) to hang her grandmother's coat.

21. Several countries are currently experiencing the horrors of (gorilla / guerrilla) warfare.

22. The (suite / sweet) at the hotel that we stayed in was beautifully decorated.

23. As the bell (told / tolled), all the villagers rushed out to see what was happening.

24. "All (hale / hail) mighty Caesar!" roared the crowds in the Colosseum.

25. I cannot stand spoilt children who (whine / wine) all the time.

26. Mr Lawrence (mowed / mode) his lawn last Saturday, but it still looks a mess.

27. The molten (lava / larva) rolled down the hillside in great fiery waves.

28. Furniture in the eighteenth century was often (guilt / gilt) with gold leaf.

29. That's not Cindy and Alex's car; (they're / their) car is parked in the next street.

30. The (lone / loan) wolf slunk through the forest, revelling in his solitude.

31. "I would not (council / counsel) such action," said the vizier to his sultan.

32. The police have closed the (borders / boarders) to prevent the criminals from escaping.

33. A great (hoard / horde) of trolls emerged out of the forest and attacked the city.

34. "This won't (lessen / lesson) your distress, but it should teach you something," said Ida.

35. "Have you seen the latest TV (ads / adds) for Christmas?" asked Will. "They're terrible!"

36. Georgio wished only to be a scholar, but the (Fêtes / Fates) had other plans for him.

37. Every day, Keira runs at least five (laps / lapse) around the park.

38. Please make sure your clothes are put on their (hangars / hangers).

39. When you have finished that orange, throw the (peel / peal) in the food recycling bin.

40. "Here. Have some of this fruit juice," said Fred. "It'll (whet / wet) your appetite."

41. My aunt lives on the thirtieth (storey / story) of a skyscraper in New York.

See how well you remember the correct spellings of the words in Units 25-29! In all of the following tests, show whether each word is correct or incorrect.

*Examples:* hello ☑
wellcome ☒

## TEST 30.1

1. abbott ☐
2. bizzare ☐
3. complient ☐
4. cargoe's ☐
5. disadvantage ☐
6. discontinued ☐
7. emperess ☐
8. extraordinary ☐
9. fourward ☐
10. giraffes ☐
11. head-master ☐
12. idealistically ☐
13. imminnent ☐
14. increese ☐
15. inconsistant ☐
16. indicies ☐
17. jabbed ☐
18. manservant ☐
19. offsprings ☐
20. potatoes ☐

SCORE _____ /20

## TEST 30.2

1. alms ☐
2. borne ☐
3. calypsoes ☐
4. disagreemant ☐
5. discolor ☐
6. droan ☐
7. exclaim ☐
8. handkerchieves ☐
9. improbably ☐
10. indistinct ☐
11. infomation ☐
12. inhibit ☐
13. interlaced ☐
14. lamma ☐
15. mattresses ☐
16. miscalculate ☐
17. oural ☐
18. pronoun ☐
19. quartes ☐
20. realloccated ☐

SCORE _____ /20

## TEST 30.3

1. allies ☐
2. alleys ☐
3. bison ☐
4. consequencial ☐
5. clothes ☐
6. disbelief ☐
7. dutchess ☐
8. external ☐
9. hieress ☐
10. ill-adviced ☐
11. inperceptable ☐
12. inequality ☐
13. invention ☐
14. marquiss ☐
15. misdiagnose ☐
16. nostrils ☐
17. occuppancy ☐
18. puffs ☐
19. rebuilt ☐
20. redoubbling ☐

SCORE _____ /20

## TEST 30.4

1. abley ☐
2. bookworms ☐
3. completetion ☐
4. comandoes ☐
5. disarm ☐
6. exclude ☐
7. eeriely ☐
8. gorrilla ☐
9. heroine ☐
10. inproper ☐
11. inaccessable ☐
12. inconsiderate ☐
13. mode ☐
14. misfire ☐
15. oboes ☐
16. pact ☐
17. reassurrence ☐
18. radishes ☐
19. barraks ☐
20. supervision ☐
21. theire ☐
22. uncharacteristic ☐

SCORE _____ /22

## TEST 30.5

1. automatic ☐
2. abbess ☐
3. chiseling ☐
4. cottages ☐
5. dishonour ☐
6. echos ☐
7. fianncée ☐
8. gnomes ☐
9. inadmissable ☐
10. indefinable ☐
11. irreconcilible ☐
12. luxiuries ☐
13. misdial ☐
14. navell ☐
15. plodder ☐
16. redeliver ☐
17. refill ☐
18. spinister ☐
19. tangos ☐
20. undrinkable ☐
21. unensured ☐
22. vixen ☐

SCORE _____ /22

## TEST 30.6

1. beliefs ☐
2. councel ☐
3. chefs ☐
4. disown ☐
5. disaprovingly ☐
6. extract ☐
7. gilt ☐
8. inpersonated ☐
9. inducible ☐
10. inexperience ☐
11. irredemeable ☐
12. mettle ☐
13. misplaced ☐
14. ourselfs ☐
15. proffess ☐
16. reevaluation ☐
17. rooster ☐
18. stake ☐
19. subscript ☐
20. tiles ☐
21. unproffesional ☐
22. urgence ☐

SCORE _____ /22

## TEST 30.7

1.  anchoves ☐
2.  bookshelves ☐
3.  course ☐
4.  children ☐
5.  disqualify ☐
6.  gander ☐
7.  hangars ☐
8.  inanimate ☐
9.  ineffective ☐
10. irrelevence ☐
11. irreverrent ☐
12. matchsticks ☐
13. proactive ☐
14. reapplied ☐
15. rythymes ☐
16. storey ☐
17. swat ☐
18. troup ☐
19. uninterrested ☐
20. unadvertised ☐
21. waiteress ☐
22. widower ☐

SCORE _____ /22

## TEST 30.8

1.  aural ☐
2.  boarders ☐
3.  contract ☐
4.  complexes ☐
5.  disregarded ☐
6.  expose ☐
7.  godess ☐
8.  hoaxes ☐
9.  imprisonmment ☐
10. inaproppriate ☐
11. inconsistancy ☐
12. irreparable ☐
13. misgovernment ☐
14. obssession ☐
15. persuasion ☐
16. sultan ☐
17. theyr'e ☐
18. thiefs ☐
19. uninvited ☐
20. unfashionable ☐
21. unemploymence ☐
22. whine ☐

SCORE _____ /22

## TEST 30.9

1.  absorebent ☐
2.  bridegroom ☐
3.  convert ☐
4.  disatissfied ☐
5.  dual ☐
6.  emperor ☐
7.  extracurricula ☐
8.  forword ☐
9.  guidence ☐
10. incouragement ☐
11. inaudible ☐
12. iritation ☐
13. lessen ☐
14. mouthes ☐
15. presidential ☐
16. suitte ☐
17. stewerd ☐
18. subdivision ☐
19. tolled ☐
20. torpedoes ☐
21. unbearable ☐
22. warlock ☐

SCORE _____ /22

## TEST 30.10

1. actress ☐
2. axes ☐
3. bazaar ☐
4. bossess ☐
5. classifiable ☐
6. crescendos ☐
7. disturbancy ☐
8. forensically ☐
9. hoarde ☐
10. inelegible ☐
11. insigniffcance ☐
12. ireplaceable ☐
13. laps ☐
14. mowed ☐
15. misremmembered ☐
16. persceptible ☐
17. rhinocerii ☐
18. succession ☐
19. trecked ☐
20. unremarkabley ☐
21. unpatriotical ☐
22. widow ☐

SCORE _____ /22

## TEST 30.11

1. autonymous ☐
2. borders ☐
3. coherrence ☐
4. chiefs ☐
5. disrespectfull ☐
6. floging ☐
7. guerrilla ☐
8. hangers ☐
9. hysterically ☐
10. inprudence ☐
11. mosquitoe ☐
12. prologue ☐
13. quartz ☐
14. sultana ☐
15. their's ☐
16. transfering ☐
17. unacknowledged ☐
18. ungramatical ☐
19. unrepentent ☐
20. unresolveble ☐
21. waltszes ☐
22. wreek ☐

SCORE _____ /22

## TEST 30.12

1. archipelagoes ☐
2. bachelour ☐
3. confectionerie ☐
4. conscientious ☐
5. differed ☐
6. disoreiented ☐
7. erossion ☐
8. extraterrestral ☐
9. fêtes's ☐
10. intervene ☐
11. irretrievable ☐
12. naval ☐
13. proficieancy ☐
14. rhetoritian ☐
15. shephardess ☐
16. subcontinent ☐
17. superscede ☐
18. transgression ☐
19. unabridged ☐
20. uncomprommising ☐
21. whet ☐
22. zeroes ☐

SCORE _____ /22

## UNIT 1

**(1)** tomorrow
**(2)** Forty
**(3)** criticises
**(4)** identity
**(5)** variety
**(6)** probably
**(7)** awkward
**(8)** occupied
**(9)** developing
**(10)** familiar
**(11)** relevant
**(12)** amateur
**(13)** harassed
**(14)** definite
**(15)** twelfth
**(16)** Wednesday
**(17)** attached
**(18)** category
**(19)** bruised
**(20)** wonderful

**(21) - (30)** *The 10 incorrectly spelt words and their correct spellings are as follows:*
occassion ⇨ occasion
parliment ⇨ parliament
dictionery ⇨ dictionary
explaination ⇨ explanation
embarass ⇨ embarrass
programe ⇨ programme
compitition ⇨ competition
corespond ⇨ correspond
nieghbour ⇨ neighbour
secretry ⇨ secretary

**(31)** × ⇨ necessary

**(32)** × ⇨ government
**(33)** × ⇨ pronunciation
**(34)** × ⇨ temperature
**(35)** ✓
**(36)** × ⇨ vegetable
**(37)** ✓
**(38)** × ⇨ restaurant
**(39)** ✓

**(40)** × (⇨ disappear)
**(41)** × (⇨ strength)
**(42)** ✓
**(43)** × (⇨ medicine)
**(44)** × (⇨ exercise)
**(45)** ✓
**(46)** ✓
**(47)** ✓
**(48)** × (⇨ address)
**(49)** × (⇨ calendar)
**(50)** × (⇨ separate)
**(51)** × (⇨ ordinary)
**(52)** ✓
**(53)** ✓
**(54)** × (⇨ particular)
**(55)** × (⇨ height)
**(56)** ✓
**(57)** ✓
**(58)** ✓
**(59)** × (⇨ favourite)
**(60)** ✓
**(61)** ✓
**(62)** ✓
**(63)** × (⇨ through OR thorough)
**(64)** ✓
**(65)** × (⇨ surprise)
**(66)** ✓
**(67)** × (⇨ remember)
**(68)** ✓
**(69)** ✓
**(70)** × (⇨ decide)
**(71)** ✓
**(72)** × (⇨ perhaps)
**(73)** ✓
**(74)** × (⇨ century)
**(75)** × (⇨ interest)
**(76)** ✓
**(77)** × (⇨ therefore)
**(78)** × (⇨ sentence)
**(79)** × (⇨ grammar)
**(80)** ✓
**(81)** ✓

**(82)** controvesy (⇨ controversy)
**(83)** determinacion (⇨ determination)
**(84)** interupted (⇨ interrupted)
**(85)** reccomend (⇨ recommend)
**(86)** Curiousity (⇨ Curiosity)
**(87)** sacrafice (⇨ sacrifice)
**(88)** prejuidice (⇨ prejudice)
**(89)** Febuary (⇨ February)
**(90)** desprately (⇨ desperately)
**(91)** comittee (⇨ committee)
**(92)** accompniament (⇨ accompaniment)
**(93)** arguement (⇨ argument)
**(94)** Eight (⇨ Eighth)
**(95)** langages (⇨ languages)
**(96)** occurences (⇨ occurrences)
**(97)** comunication (⇨ communication)
**(98)** enviroment (⇨ environment)
**(99)** actuall (⇨ actual)
**(100)** sinscerity (⇨ sincerity)

**(101)** All 3 are correct
**(102)** shoulder
**(103)** knowledge
**(104)** complete
**(105)** continue
**(106)** All 3 are incorrect
**(107)** describe; frequently
**(108)** All 3 are incorrect
**(109)** expertise
**(110)** develop; soldier
**(111)** parallel
**(112)** material
**(113)** All 3 are correct
**(114)** All 3 are incorrect
**(115)** rhyme; thought

**(116)** B. woman ... breath
**(117)** C. questions ... difficult
**(118)** D. increase ... busy
**(119)** A. arrive ... early
**(120)** C. guide ... promised
**(121)** B. enough ... pressure
**(122)** D. notice ... opposite
**(123)** A. regular ... occasionally
**(124)** C. positions ... though

## UNIT 2

**(1)** reincarnation
**(2)** coincide
**(3)** anti-inflammatory
**(4)** co-operation

**(5)** reimburse
**(6)** collaborate
**(7)** de-emphasise
**(8)** deduce
**(9)** antihero OR anti-hero
**(10)** re-employ
**(11)** recurring
**(12)** semicircle
**(13)** reduce
**(14)** collision
**(15)** redeem

**(16)** re-enter
**(17)** co-ordination
**(18)** semi-automatic OR semiautomatic
**(19)** redesigned
**(20)** microbiologist
**(21)** de-escalate
**(22)** re-editing
**(23)** antibodies
**(24)** co-organisers
**(25)** semicolon
**(26)** demoted
**(27)** re-examining
**(28)** antisocial
**(29)** re-elected
**(30)** co-operate
**(31)** micro-organism

## UNIT 3

**(1)** fr__nd ⇨ friend
**(2)** l__sure ⇨ leisure
**(3)** anx__ty ⇨ anxiety
**(4)** conven__nt ⇨ convenient
**(5)** r__gn ⇨ reign
**(6)** fr__ght ⇨ freight
**(7)** for__gn ⇨ foreign
**(8)** __derdown ⇨ eiderdown
**(9)** impat__nt ⇨ impatient
**(10)** br__fcase ⇨ briefcase
**(11)** w__ght ⇨ weight
**(12)** n__ghbourhood ⇨ neighbourhood
**(13)** y__ld ⇨ yield
**(14)** r__ndeer ⇨ reindeer
**(15)** sover__gn ⇨ sovereign
**(16)** hyg__ne ⇨ hygiene
**(17)** gondol__r ⇨ gondolier

**(18)** ✓
**(19)** ✗ (releived ⇨ relieved)
**(20)** ✗ (siezed ⇨ seized)

**(21)** ✗ (beseiged ⇨ besieged)
**(22)** ✓
**(23)** ✓
**(24)** ✗ (unvieling ⇨ unveiling)
**(25)** ✗ (ingredeint ⇨ ingredient)
**(26)** ✓
**(27)** ✗ (leneint ⇨ lenient)
**(28)** ✓
**(29)** ✗ (lieutenant ⇨ lieutenant)
**(30)** ✗ (chandeleir ⇨ chandelier)
**(31)** ✓
**(32)** ✗ (neice ⇨ niece)
**(33)** ✓
**(34)** ✗ (well-recieved ⇨ well-received)
**(35)** ✗ (biege ⇨ beige)

## UNIT 4

**(1)** A. cautious ... tiptoed
**(2)** D. vicious ... defenceless
**(3)** B. sailor ... precious
**(4)** D. Nutritious ... unappetising
**(5)** A. boring ... repetitious
**(6)** C. nonsense ... fictitious
**(7)** B. ambitious ... monotonous
**(8)** C. spacious ... luxurious
**(9)** D. voracious ... atrocious

**(10)** curious
**(11)** All 3 are correct
**(12)** anxious; suspicious
**(13)** superstitious; hideous
**(14)** dangerous; perilous
**(15)** conscious
**(16)** All 3 are incorrect
**(17)** tremendous; jealous
**(18)** All 3 are correct
**(19)** tedious; joyous
**(20)** All 3 are correct
**(21)** venomous
**(22)** ridiculous
**(23)** All 3 are incorrect
**(24)** All 3 are incorrect

## UNIT 5

**(1)** A. essential
**(2)** C. confidential
**(3)** D. artificial
**(4)** A. officials
**(5)** B. provincial
**(6)** C. special
**(7)** C. residential

**(8)** A. glacial
**(9)** D. social
**(10)** B. infomercials

**(11)** s u p e r f i c i a l
**(12)** f i n a n c i a l
**(13)** p a r t i a l
**(14)** c o m m e r c i a l
**(15)** p o t e n t i a l
**(16)** s e q u e n t i a l
**(17)** r a c i a l
**(18)** p a l a t i a l
**(19)** c r u c i a l
**(20)** i n f l u e n t i a l
**(21)** e s p e c i a l
**(22)** m a r t i a l
**(23)** i m p a r t i a l
**(24)** f a c i a l
**(25)** u n o f f i c i a l
**(26)** b e n e f i c i a l
**(27)** j u d i c i a l
**(28)** s u b s t a n t i a l

## UNIT 6

### TEST 6.1

| | | |
|---|---|---|
| **(1)** ✓ | **(8)** ✗ | **(15)** ✗ |
| **(2)** ✗ | **(9)** ✓ | **(16)** ✗ |
| **(3)** ✗ | **(10)** ✓ | **(17)** ✗ |
| **(4)** ✓ | **(11)** ✗ | **(18)** ✓ |
| **(5)** ✗ | **(12)** ✓ | **(19)** ✗ |
| **(6)** ✗ | **(13)** ✓ | **(20)** ✓ |
| **(7)** ✗ | **(14)** ✓ | |

*(2)* awkward; *(3)* barbarous; *(5)* complete; *(6)* deduce; *(7)* excellent; *(8)* grieved; *(11)* occasion; *(15)* sacrifice; *(16)* suspicious; *(17)* twelfth; *(19)* variety

### TEST 6.2

| | | |
|---|---|---|
| **(1)** ✗ | **(8)** ✓ | **(15)** ✗ |
| **(2)** ✗ | **(9)** ✓ | **(16)** ✗ |
| **(3)** ✓ | **(10)** ✗ | **(17)** ✗ |
| **(4)** ✓ | **(11)** ✓ | **(18)** ✓ |
| **(5)** ✗ | **(12)** ✗ | **(19)** ✗ |
| **(6)** ✓ | **(13)** ✓ | **(20)** ✗ |
| **(7)** ✗ | **(14)** ✗ | |

(1) accompany; (2) average; (5) confidential; (7) exercise; (10) malicious; (12) particular; (14) relevant; (15) redeem; (16) scientific; (17) surprise; (19) tremendous; (20) vigorous

(1) ambitious; (2) argument; (3) besieged; (5) convenience; (6) disappear; (7) existence; (9) hazardous; (10) infamous; (13) ordinary; (19) sovereign; (21) unveiling; (22) well-received

| (6) × | (14) × | (22) ✓ |
| (7) ✓ | (15) ✓ | |
| (8) × | (16) ✓ | |

(5) counterfeit; (6) desperately; (8) eighth; (9) forwards; (10) humongous; (11) infomercials; (12) luxurious; (13) mountainous; (14) peculiar; (18) repetitious; (19) sincerely; (20) signature; (21) tomorrow

## TEST 6.3

| (1) × | (8) × | (15) ✓ |
|---|---|---|
| (2) ✓ | (9) ✓ | (16) × |
| (3) × | (10) × | (17) ✓ |
| (4) ✓ | (11) ✓ | (18) × |
| (5) × | (12) ✓ | (19) ✓ |
| (6) × | (13) × | (20) × |
| (7) ✓ | (14) ✓ | |

## TEST 6.6

| (1) ✓ | (9) × | (17) × |
|---|---|---|
| (2) × | (10) ✓ | (18) ✓ |
| (3) ✓ | (11) ✓ | (19) ✓ |
| (4) × | (12) × | (20) ✓ |
| (5) ✓ | (13) × | (21) × |
| (6) ✓ | (14) × | (22) ✓ |
| (7) ✓ | (15) ✓ | |
| (8) × | (16) × | |

## TEST 6.9

| (1) × | (9) ✓ | (17) × |
|---|---|---|
| (2) ✓ | (10) × | (18) × |
| (3) × | (11) × | (19) × |
| (4) ✓ | (12) × | (20) × |
| (5) × | (13) ✓ | (21) ✓ |
| (6) × | (14) ✓ | (22) × |
| (7) × | (15) × | |
| (8) × | (16) ✓ | |

(1) adventurous; (3) believe; (5) curiosity; (6) desperate; (8) February; (10) impatient; (13) niece; (16) precious; (18) redesigned; (20) weird

(2) atrocious; (4) coincide; (8) financial; (9) herbivorous; (12) lieutenant; (13) minute; (14) possession; (16) rhythm; (17) re-enter; (21) superstitious

(1) antihero; (3) brigadier; (5) conscious; (6) disastrous; (7) equipment; (8) especially; (10) government; (11) hygiene; (12) ingredient; (15) perilous; (17) rhyme; (18) restaurant; (19) re-examining; (20) secretary; (22) thunderous

## TEST 6.4

| (1) ✓ | (9) ✓ | (17) × |
|---|---|---|
| (2) ✓ | (10) × | (18) ✓ |
| (3) × | (11) ✓ | (19) ✓ |
| (4) ✓ | (12) ✓ | (20) ✓ |
| (5) ✓ | (13) × | (21) × |
| (6) ✓ | (14) × | (22) × |
| (7) × | (15) ✓ | |
| (8) × | (16) ✓ | |

## TEST 6.7

| (1) × | (9) × | (17) ✓ |
|---|---|---|
| (2) × | (10) × | (18) ✓ |
| (3) ✓ | (11) ✓ | (19) ✓ |
| (4) × | (12) ✓ | (20) ✓ |
| (5) × | (13) ✓ | (21) × |
| (6) × | (14) × | (22) × |
| (7) × | (15) ✓ | |
| (8) ✓ | (16) × | |

## TEST 6.10

| (1) × | (9) × | (17) ✓ |
|---|---|---|
| (2) × | (10) ✓ | (18) × |
| (3) × | (11) ✓ | (19) × |
| (4) × | (12) × | (20) ✓ |
| (5) ✓ | (13) ✓ | (21) × |
| (6) ✓ | (14) × | (22) × |
| (7) × | (15) × | |
| (8) × | (16) × | |

(3) beneficial; (5) controversy; (7) especial; (8) favourite; (10) harassed; (13) microbiologist; (14) nutritious; (17) prosperous; (21) superficial; (22) venomous

(1) amateur; (2) artificial; (4) collaborate; (5) co-ordination; (6) delicious; (7) extreme; (9) fictitious; (10) hideous; (14) micro-organism; (16) outrageous; (21) special; (22) unappetising

(1) accidentally; (2) aggressive; (3) bruised; (4) committee; (7) determination; (8) environment; (9) explanation; (12) necessary; (14) programme; (15) recurring; (16) reindeer; (18) spacious; (19) substantial; (21) therefore; (22) Wednesday

## TEST 6.5

| (1) × | (9) × | (17) ✓ |
|---|---|---|
| (2) × | (10) × | (18) ✓ |
| (3) × | (11) ✓ | (19) × |
| (4) ✓ | (12) ✓ | (20) ✓ |
| (5) × | (13) × | (21) ✓ |
| (6) × | (14) ✓ | (22) × |
| (7) × | (15) ✓ | |
| (8) ✓ | (16) ✓ | |

## TEST 6.8

| (1) ✓ | (9) × | (17) ✓ |
|---|---|---|
| (2) ✓ | (10) × | (18) × |
| (3) ✓ | (11) × | (19) × |
| (4) ✓ | (12) × | (20) × |
| (5) × | (13) × | (21) × |

## TEST 6.11

| | | |
|---|---|---|
| **(1)** ✗ | **(9)** ✓ | **(17)** ✓ |
| **(2)** ✓ | **(10)** ✗ | **(18)** ✗ |
| **(3)** ✓ | **(11)** ✓ | **(19)** ✓ |
| **(4)** ✓ | **(12)** ✗ | **(20)** ✗ |
| **(5)** ✓ | **(13)** ✗ | **(21)** ✗ |
| **(6)** ✗ | **(14)** ✗ | **(22)** ✗ |
| **(7)** ✗ | **(15)** ✗ | |
| **(8)** ✗ | **(16)** ✓ | |

*(1) accompaniment; (6) demoted; (7) disobedient; (8) embarrass; (10) grammar; (12) occurrences; (13) parliament; (14) pretentious; (15) recommend; (18) semicolon; (20) sincerity; (21) temperature; (22) yield*

## TEST 6.12

| | | |
|---|---|---|
| **(1)** ✗ | **(9)** ✓ | **(17)** ✓ |
| **(2)** ✓ | **(10)** ✓ | **(18)** ✗ |
| **(3)** ✓ | **(11)** ✗ | **(19)** ✓ |
| **(4)** ✗ | **(12)** ✓ | **(20)** ✓ |
| **(5)** ✓ | **(13)** ✗ | **(21)** ✗ |
| **(6)** ✗ | **(14)** ✗ | **(22)** ✓ |
| **(7)** ✓ | **(15)** ✗ | |
| **(8)** ✓ | **(16)** ✗ | |

*(1) anti-inflammatory; (4) convenient; (6) decaffeinated; (11) guarantee; (13) neighbourhood; (14) occasionally; (15) poltergeist; (16) pronunciation; (18) rebellious; (21) treacherous*

## UNIT 7

**(1)** dis + courage ⇨ discourage
**(2)** mis + lead ⇨ mislead
**(3)** ir + relevant ⇨ irrelevant
**(4)** mis + behave ⇨ misbehave
**(5)** dis + possess ⇨ dispossess
**(6)** mis + print ⇨ misprint
**(7)** mis + address ⇨ misaddress
**(8)** ir + regular ⇨ irregular
**(9)** dis + obey ⇨ disobey
**(10)** mis + govern ⇨ misgovern
**(11)** il + legal ⇨ illegal
**(12)** dis + count ⇨ discount OR
mis + count ⇨ miscount
**(13)** dis + agree ⇨ disagree
**(14)** mis + guide ⇨ misguide
**(15)** mis + heard ⇨ misheard
**(16)** dis + appoint ⇨ disappoint
**(17)** il + legible ⇨ illegible
**(18)** ir + rational ⇨ irrational
**(19)** dis + allow ⇨ disallow
**(20)** dis + regard ⇨ disregard OR
mis + regard ⇨ misregard
**(21)** dis + pose ⇨ dispose
**(22)** mis + fit ⇨ misfit
**(23)** mis + shaped ⇨ misshaped
**(24)** dis + arm ⇨ disarm
**(25)** dis + able ⇨ disable
**(26)** mis + align ⇨ misalign
**(27)** mis + conduct ⇨ misconduct
**(28)** dis + card ⇨ discard
**(29)** dis + grace ⇨ disgrace
**(30)** dis + honest ⇨ dishonest
**(31)** mis + handle ⇨ mishandle
**(32)** mis + label ⇨ mislabel

**(33)** illiterate
**(34)** disapproval
**(35)** misspelled OR misspelt
**(36)** irresponsible
**(37)** disappearance
**(38)** misremember
**(39)** dissatisfied
**(40)** discontinuing
**(41)** mistreatment
**(42)** disadvantage
**(43)** disagreeable
**(44)** illogical
**(45)** mistrustful
**(46)** irresistible
**(47)** disappointment
**(48)** misapprehension
**(49)** misdeed
**(50)** irreversible
**(51)** mislaid
**(52)** disembarked
**(53)** discourteous
**(54)** misdirection
**(55)** disassemble
**(56)** discomfort
**(57)** misinformation
**(58)** disenchanted
**(59)** misconception
**(60)** dissimilarity
**(61)** misapplied
**(62)** disruption
**(63)** misspeak
**(64)** disorderly
**(65)** misjudged
**(66)** dismissal
**(67)** illegitimate
**(68)** disbelievingly

## UNIT 8

**(1)** ✗ ⇨ conceive
**(2)** ✗ ⇨ mischievous
**(3)** ✓
**(4)** ✓
**(5)** ✗ ⇨ ceiling
**(6)** ✓
**(7)** ✓
**(8)** ✓
**(9)** ✗ ⇨ juiciest
**(10)** ✗ ⇨ concierge
**(11)** ✓
**(12)** ✗ ⇨ receipts
**(13)** ✓
**(14)** ✗ ⇨ financier
**(15)** ✗ ⇨ piercingly
**(16)** ✓
**(17)** ✗ ⇨ recipes
**(18)** ✓
**(19)** ✓
**(20)** ✗ ⇨ transceivers
**(21)** ✗ ⇨ conceitedness
**(22)** ✓

## UNIT 9

**(1)** charity
**(2)** psyche
**(3)** crescent
**(4)** cyanide
**(5)** enchilada
**(6)** rye
**(7)** martyr
**(8)** crescendo
**(9)** archipelago
**(10)** gyroscope
**(11)** fluorescent

**(12)** ✗ (⇨ asymmetrical)
**(13)** ✓
**(14)** ✗ (⇨ schemes)
**(15)** ✗ (⇨ isosceles)
**(16)** ✓
**(17)** ✓
**(18)** ✗ (⇨ echoing)
**(19)** ✗ (⇨ Chrysanthemums)
**(20)** ✗ (⇨ scenery)

(21) ✗ (⇨ platypus)
(22) ✓
(23) ✗ (⇨ architect)
(24) ✗ (⇨ susceptible)
(25) ✗ (⇨ sceptre)
(26) ✓
(27) ✓
(28) ✓
(29) ✗ (⇨ scholar)
(30) ✗ (⇨ hierarchical)

(31) chef
(32) tongue
(33) moustache
(34) unique
(35) machine
(36) League
(37) brochure
(38) parachute
(39) chalet
(40) antique
(41) colleagues
(42) boutique
(43) plague
(44) chivalry
(45) bouquet
(46) chandelier
(47) catalogue
(48) pistachio
(49) cheque

(50) picturesque
(51) champagne
(52) racquet
(53) physique
(54) fuchsia
(55) grotesque
(56) arachnid
(57) question
(58) archive
(59) chasm
(60) opaque

## UNIT 10

(1) democratic + ally ⇨ democratically
(2) separate + ly ⇨ separately
(3) harsh + ly ⇨ harshly
(4) grave + ly ⇨ gravely
(5) Begrudging + ly ⇨ Begrudgingly
(6) literal + ly ⇨ literally
(7) flimsy + ly ⇨ flimsily

(8) magic + ally ⇨ magically
(9) naive + ly ⇨ naively
(10) persuasive + ly ⇨ persuasively
(11) complete + ly ⇨ completely
(12) abominable + ly ⇨ abominably
(13) ready + ly ⇨ readily
(14) Historic + ally ⇨ Historically
(15) Ordinary + ly ⇨ Ordinarily
(16) precise + ly ⇨ precisely
(17) cryptic + ally ⇨ cryptically
(18) hoarse + ly ⇨ hoarsely
(19) environment + ally ⇨ environmentally

(20) D. miserably
(21) B. basically
(22) C. immediately
(23) A. cheerily
(24) C. inexplicably
(25) D. pompously
(26) B. academically
(27) D. temporarily
(28) A. tangibly
(29) C. elaborately

## UNIT 11

(1) prevent + able ⇨ preventable
(2) envy + able ⇨ enviable
(3) apply + able ⇨ applicable
(4) mention + able ⇨ mentionable
(5) adore + able ⇨ adorable
(6) question + able ⇨ questionable
(7) admit + ible ⇨ admissible
(8) reverse + ible ⇨ reversible
(9) like + able ⇨ likeable
(10) answer + able ⇨ answerable
(11) construct + able OR ible ⇨ constructable OR constructible
(12) imagine + able ⇨ imaginable
(13) deny + able ⇨ deniable
(14) attach + able ⇨ attachable
(15) deduce + ible ⇨ deducible
(16) regret + able ⇨ regrettable
(17) knowledge + able ⇨ knowledgeable
(18) recommend + able ⇨ recommendable

(19) programme + able ⇨ programmable
(20) achieve + able ⇨ achievable
(21) vary + able ⇨ variable
(22) access + ible ⇨ accessible
(23) breathe + able ⇨ breathable
(24) suggest + ible ⇨ suggestible
(25) collapse + ible ⇨ collapsible
(26) destruct + ible ⇨ destructible
(27) tolerate + able ⇨ tolerable
(28) suppose + able ⇨ supposable
(29) divide + ible ⇨ divisible
(30) consume + able ⇨ consumable
(31) collect + ible ⇨ collectible
(32) appreciate + able ⇨ appreciable

(33) C. conclusion ... debatable
(34) B. damage ... considerably
(35) D. suggestion ... sensibly
(36) A. comfortable ... purchase
(37) D. legible ... impossible
(38) B. reliable ... changeable
(39) C. forcible ... persuadable
(40) C. dependably ... enjoyable
(41) A. noticeably ... understandable

## UNIT 12

### TEST 12.1

| | | |
|---|---|---|
| (1) ✗ | (8) ✓ | (15) ✓ |
| (2) ✓ | (9) ✗ | (16) ✓ |
| (3) ✓ | (10) ✓ | (17) ✓ |
| (4) ✓ | (11) ✓ | (18) ✓ |
| (5) ✓ | (12) ✗ | (19) ✓ |
| (6) ✗ | (13) ✗ | (20) ✓ |
| (7) ✗ | (14) ✗ | |

*(1) achievable; (6) colleagues; (7) disable; (9) elaborately; (12) immediately; (13) juiciest (14) literal*

## TEST 12.2

| | | |
|---|---|---|
| (1) ✗ | (8) ✗ | (15) ✗ |
| (2) ✓ | (9) ✓ | (16) ✓ |
| (3) ✗ | (10) ✓ | (17) ✓ |
| (4) ✓ | (11) ✓ | (18) ✗ |
| (5) ✓ | (12) ✓ | (19) ✗ |
| (6) ✗ | (13) ✗ | (20) ✗ |
| (7) ✗ | (14) ✓ | |

*(1)* acces*si*ble; *(3)* ban*q*uet; *(6)* champ*ag*ne; *(7)* disa*g*ree; *(8)* discou*r*age; *(13)* i*ll*ogical; *(15)* mischie*v*ous; *(18)* per*s*uasive; *(19)* ra*c*quet; *(20)* scept*re*

## TEST 12.3

| | | |
|---|---|---|
| (1) ✗ | (8) ✗ | (15) ✗ |
| (2) ✗ | (9) ✓ | (16) ✗ |
| (3) ✗ | (10) ✗ | (17) ✓ |
| (4) ✗ | (11) ✓ | (18) ✗ |
| (5) ✗ | (12) ✗ | (19) ✗ |
| (6) ✓ | (13) ✗ | (20) ✓ |
| (7) ✓ | (14) ✗ | |

*(1)* ab*o*minable; *(2)* begrud*g*ing; *(3)* conc*ei*ve; *(4)* collec*ti*ble; *(5)* chand*e*lier; *(8)* di*s*appoint; *(10)* fi*n*ancier; *(12)* i*rr*ational; *(13)* lea*g*ue; *(14)* mis*f*it; *(15)* mis*s*pelt; *(16)* miser*a*bly; *(18)* pierc*i*ngly; *(19)* para*c*hute

## TEST 12.4

| | | |
|---|---|---|
| (1) ✓ | (9) ✓ | (17) ✗ |
| (2) ✗ | (10) ✗ | (18) ✓ |
| (3) ✓ | (11) ✓ | (19) ✗ |
| (4) ✓ | (12) ✓ | (20) ✗ |
| (5) ✗ | (13) ✓ | (21) ✗ |
| (6) ✗ | (14) ✗ | (22) ✓ |
| (7) ✗ | (15) ✗ | |
| (8) ✗ | (16) ✓ | |

*(2)* avalanch*e*; *(5)* choru*s*; *(6)* charac*t*er; *(7)* dec*ei*vers; *(8)* di*s*appearance; *(10)* enjoy*a*ble; *(14)* mi*s*applied; *(15)* men*ti*on*a*ble; *(17)* pla*g*ue;

*(19)* sch*e*me; *(20)* sque*lch*; *(21)* to*l*erable

## TEST 12.5

| | | |
|---|---|---|
| (1) ✗ | (9) ✓ | (17) ✓ |
| (2) ✓ | (10) ✗ | (18) ✗ |
| (3) ✗ | (11) ✗ | (19) ✗ |
| (4) ✓ | (12) ✓ | (20) ✓ |
| (5) ✓ | (13) ✗ | (21) ✓ |
| (6) ✗ | (14) ✗ | (22) ✗ |
| (7) ✗ | (15) ✗ | |
| (8) ✓ | (16) ✓ | |

*(1)* admi*ss*ible; *(3)* consu*m*able; *(6)* dedu*ci*ble; *(7)* di*s*approval; *(10)* gym*n*asium; *(11)* inexpli*c*ably; *(13)* misinfor*m*ation; *(14)* misla*i*d; *(15)* mis*s*peak; *(18)* regre*tt*able; *(19)* socie*ti*es; *(22)* scen*e*ry

## TEST 12.6

| | | |
|---|---|---|
| (1) ✗ | (9) ✓ | (17) ✓ |
| (2) ✗ | (10) ✓ | (18) ✗ |
| (3) ✗ | (11) ✓ | (19) ✗ |
| (4) ✗ | (12) ✗ | (20) ✓ |
| (5) ✓ | (13) ✓ | (21) ✗ |
| (6) ✗ | (14) ✓ | (22) ✗ |
| (7) ✗ | (15) ✓ | |
| (8) ✓ | (16) ✓ | |

*(1)* ador*a*ble; *(2)* appre*ci*ate; *(3)* cryp*ti*c; *(4)* comfort*a*ble; *(6)* dem*o*cratic; *(7)* di*s*assemble; *(12)* i*ll*iterate; *(18)* readi*l*y; *(19)* se*p*arate; *(21)* syno*n*ym; *(22)* transc*ei*vers

## TEST 12.7

| | | |
|---|---|---|
| (1) ✓ | (9) ✓ | (17) ✗ |
| (2) ✗ | (10) ✓ | (18) ✓ |
| (3) ✗ | (11) ✗ | (19) ✓ |
| (4) ✗ | (12) ✗ | (20) ✗ |
| (5) ✗ | (13) ✓ | (21) ✓ |
| (6) ✗ | (14) ✗ | (22) ✗ |
| (7) ✗ | (15) ✗ | |
| (8) ✓ | (16) ✓ | |

*(2)* a*q*ueduct; *(3)* collap*si*ble; *(4)* con*sci*ence; *(5)* chape*r*one; *(6)* deni*a*ble; *(7)* di*s*missal; *(11)* i*rr*esponsible; *(14)* mous*t*ache; *(15)* mis*s*haped; *(17)* persuad*a*ble; *(20)* suppo*s*able; *(22)* tan*gi*bly

## TEST 12.8

| | | |
|---|---|---|
| (1) ✗ | (9) ✓ | (17) ✗ |
| (2) ✓ | (10) ✗ | (18) ✓ |
| (3) ✗ | (11) ✗ | (19) ✗ |
| (4) ✓ | (12) ✓ | (20) ✓ |
| (5) ✗ | (13) ✓ | (21) ✗ |
| (6) ✗ | (14) ✓ | (22) ✓ |
| (7) ✓ | (15) ✗ | |
| (8) ✓ | (16) ✓ | |

*(1)* appli*c*able; *(3)* conc*ie*rge; *(5)* charismatic; *(6)* destruc*ti*ble; *(10)* ir*r*elevant; *(11)* knowledg*e*able; *(15)* prevent*a*ble; *(17)* recommend*a*ble; *(19)* tech*ni*que; *(21)* tempo*r*arily

## TEST 12.9

| | | |
|---|---|---|
| (1) ✗ | (9) ✗ | (17) ✓ |
| (2) ✓ | (10) ✗ | (18) ✗ |
| (3) ✓ | (11) ✗ | (19) ✗ |
| (4) ✓ | (12) ✗ | (20) ✗ |
| (5) ✗ | (13) ✗ | (21) ✗ |
| (6) ✗ | (14) ✓ | (22) ✓ |
| (7) ✗ | (15) ✗ | |
| (8) ✓ | (16) ✓ | |

*(1)* appreci*a*ble; *(5)* ch*e*que; *(6)* cha*uff*eur; *(7)* di*s*appointment; *(9)* divi*si*ble; *(10)* fl*uo*rescent; *(11)* gyr*o*scope; *(12)* ir*r*esistible; *(13)* illega*l*; *(15)* mistrustful; *(18)* pla*q*ue; *(19)* sen*si*bly; *(20)* tympan*i*; *(21)* unperce*iv*ed

## TEST 12.10

| | | |
|---|---|---|
| (1) ✓ | (9) ✓ | (17) ✓ |
| (2) ✓ | (10) ✗ | (18) ✓ |
| (3) ✓ | (11) ✓ | (19) ✗ |
| (4) ✓ | (12) ✓ | (20) ✗ |

(5) ×    (13) ×    (21) ×
(6) ✓    (14) ×    (22) ✓
(7) ×    (15) ✓
(8) ×    (16) ✓

(5) considerably; (7) damage; (8) deficiency; (10) dispossess; (13) historically; (14) irreversible; (19) programmable; (20) psyche; (21) recipes

## TEST 12.11

(1) ✓    (9) ✓    (17) ×
(2) ×    (10) ×    (18) ✓
(3) ×    (11) ×    (19) ×
(4) ✓    (12) ✓    (20) ×
(5) ✓    (13) ×    (21) ×
(6) ×    (14) ×    (22) ×
(7) ✓    (15) ✓
(8) ×    (16) ✓

(2) bronchitis; (3) catalogue; (6) debatable; (8) discontinuing; (10) dissatisfied; (11) equestrian; (13) hoarsely; (14) illegitimate; (17) pistachio; (19) queasy; (20) reversible; (21) syndicate; (22) suggestible

## TEST 12.12

(1) ×    (9) ✓    (17) ×
(2) ✓    (10) ×    (18) ×
(3) ×    (11) ×    (19) ×
(4) ×    (12) ×    (20) ×
(5) ×    (13) ×    (21) ×
(6) ×    (14) ✓    (22) ✓
(7) ×    (15) ✓
(8) ×    (16) ×

(1) abominably; (3) chrysanthemums; (4) conceitedness; (5) crèche; (6) dependably; (7) disadvantage; (8) disagreeable; (10) disembarked; (11) dissimilarity; (12) effervescent; (13) gymkhana; (16) illegible; (17) martyr; (18) misapprehension;

(19) naively; (20) omniscient; (21) photosynthesis

## UNIT 13

(1) immature
(2) inattentive
(3) incorrect
(4) imbalance
(5) inadvisable
(6) immortal
(7) impatient
(8) indefinite
(9) imprudent
(10) infamous
(11) inadequate
(12) impractical
(13) insufficient
(14) imprecise
(15) injustice
(16) invalid
(17) immoral
(18) inedible
(19) immoveable

(20) review
(21) immigrate
(22) indirect
(23) renovate
(24) implied
(25) intake
(26) rejected
(27) replay
(28) refused
(29) intersects
(30) informed
(31) imported
(32) reconnect
(33) repelled
(34) inactive
(35) intermediate
(36) incur
(37) impaired
(38) inclined

(39) inter + national ⇨ international
(40) re + decorate ⇨ redecorate
(41) im + prove ⇨ improve
(42) in + humane ⇨ inhumane
(43) in + accurate ⇨ inaccurate
(44) re + act ⇨ react OR inter + act ⇨ interact
(45) re + claim ⇨ reclaim

(46) inter + change ⇨ interchange
(47) im + polite ⇨ impolite
(48) re + acquaint ⇨ reacquaint
(49) in + formal ⇨ informal
(50) inter + city ⇨ intercity
(51) im + plant ⇨ implant OR re + plant ⇨ replant
(52) inter + library ⇨ interlibrary
(53) re + fund ⇨ refund
(54) re + consider ⇨ reconsider
(55) in + destructible ⇨ indestructible
(56) im + personal ⇨ impersonal OR inter + personal ⇨ interpersonal
(57) re + mission ⇨ remission OR inter + mission ⇨ intermission
(58) in + capable ⇨ incapable
(59) in + dignity ⇨ indignity
(60) re + boot ⇨ reboot
(61) im + mobile ⇨ immobile
(62) in + compatible ⇨ incompatible
(63) inter + twine ⇨ intertwine
(64) re + generate ⇨ regenerate
(65) in + separable ⇨ inseparable
(66) im + plausible ⇨ implausible
(67) im + material ⇨ immaterial
(68) inter + galactic ⇨ intergalactic
(69) in + conclusive ⇨ inconclusive
(70) im + pertinent ⇨ impertinent

## UNIT 14

(1) cough
(2) route
(3) vow
(4) trout
(5) cower
(6) trough
(7) rogue
(8) draught
(9) borough
(10) chart
(11) south
(12) pout
(13) throat
(14) allow

**(15)** bout
**(16)** hiccough

## UNIT 15

**(1)** doubts; b
**(2)** muscle; c
**(3)** island; s
**(4)** biscuits; u
**(5)** lamb; b
**(6)** vehicles; h
**(7)** business; i
**(8)** solemnly; n
**(9)** succumbed; b
**(10)** thistle; t
**(11)** cologne; g

**(12)** f<u>a</u>scinated
**(13)** a<u>r</u>chaeologist
**(14)** n<u>u</u>isance
**(15)** q<u>u</u>eued
**(16)** wr<u>i</u>nkled
**(17)** s<u>c</u>ent
**(18)** wr<u>e</u>ck
**(19)** r<u>h</u>ymes
**(20)** receipt
**(21)** r<u>u</u>stling
**(22)** chemica<u>l</u>s
**(23)** g<u>u</u>arantee<u>s</u>
**(24)** g<u>n</u>ashed
**(25)** p<u>n</u>eumonia
**(26)** d<u>i</u>s<u>gu</u>ise
**(27)** d<u>e</u>bt
**(28)** knapsack
**(29)** campaigning
**(30)** C<u>a</u>tacombs

## UNIT 16

**(1)** observe ⇨ observ<u>ant</u>; observ<u>ance</u>
**(2)** differ ⇨ differ<u>ent</u>; differ<u>ence</u>
**(3)** hinder ⇨ hind<u>rance</u>
**(4)** obey ⇨ obed<u>ient</u>; obed<u>ience</u>
**(5)** hesitate ⇨ hesit<u>ant</u>; hesit<u>ancy</u> OR hesit<u>ance</u>
**(6)** expect ⇨ expect<u>ant</u>; expect<u>ancy</u> OR expect<u>ance</u>
**(7)** reside ⇨ resid<u>ent</u>; resid<u>ence</u>; resid<u>ency</u>
**(8)** assist ⇨ assist<u>ant</u>; assist<u>ance</u>
**(9)** correspond ⇨ correspond<u>ent</u>; correspond<u>ence</u>
**(10)** suffice ⇨ suffic<u>ient</u>; suffic<u>iency</u>
**(11)** survey ⇨ surveill<u>ance</u>
**(12)** depend ⇨ depend<u>ant</u>; depend<u>ent</u>; depend<u>ence</u>; depend<u>ency</u>

**(13)** increm<u>ent</u> (increme<u>nce</u> ✗)
**(14)** subst<u>ance</u> (subst<u>ence</u> ✗)
**(15)** toler<u>ance</u> (toler<u>ence</u> ✗)
**(16)** independ<u>ent</u> (independ<u>ant</u> ✗)
**(17)** insist<u>ent</u> (insist<u>ant</u> ✗)
**(18)** disobed<u>ience</u> (disobed<u>eience</u> ✗)
**(19)** neglig<u>ent</u> (neglig<u>ient</u> ✗)
**(20)** recip<u>ient</u> (recip<u>iant</u> ✗)
**(21)** resil<u>ience</u> (resil<u>iance</u> ✗)
**(22)** compon<u>ent</u> (compon<u>ant</u> ✗)
**(23)** leni<u>ence</u> (leni<u>ance</u> ✗)
**(24)** incompet<u>ence</u> (incompet<u>ance</u> ✗)

## UNIT 17

**(1)** alter
**(2)** draft
**(3)** Practice
**(4)** guessed
**(5)** mourning
**(6)** Steel
**(7)** who's
**(8)** brews
**(9)** hart
**(10)** accept
**(11)** principal
**(12)** stationery
**(13)** led
**(14)** bawl
**(15)** Great
**(16)** wary
**(17)** devise
**(18)** serial
**(19)** assent
**(20)** further
**(21)** bridal
**(22)** profit
**(23)** effect
**(24)** herd
**(25)** dessert
**(26)** complements
**(27)** aisle
**(28)** proceed
**(29)** lightening
**(30)** meddle

**(31)** licence
**(32)** past
**(33)** aloud
**(34)** dissent
**(35)** prophesy
**(36)** missed
**(37)** whether
**(38)** advice
**(39)** current
**(40)** patience
**(41)** wrung

## UNIT 18

### TEST 18.1

| | | |
|---|---|---|
| **(1)** ✓ | **(8)** ✓ | **(15)** ✓ |
| **(2)** ✗ | **(9)** ✗ | **(16)** ✓ |
| **(3)** ✓ | **(10)** ✗ | **(17)** ✗ |
| **(4)** ✓ | **(11)** ✓ | **(18)** ✓ |
| **(5)** ✗ | **(12)** ✓ | **(19)** ✗ |
| **(6)** ✓ | **(13)** ✗ | **(20)** ✓ |
| **(7)** ✗ | **(14)** ✓ | |

*(2) bou<u>t</u>; (5) diff<u>er</u>ent; (7) ex<u>c</u>ept; (9) imm<u>a</u>terial; (10) impa<u>t</u>ient; (13) ine<u>ffi</u>ciency; (17) obed<u>i</u>ent; (19) res<u>i</u>dency*

### TEST 18.2

| | | |
|---|---|---|
| **(1)** ✗ | **(8)** ✗ | **(15)** ✓ |
| **(2)** ✓ | **(9)** ✓ | **(16)** ✗ |
| **(3)** ✗ | **(10)** ✗ | **(17)** ✗ |
| **(4)** ✗ | **(11)** ✗ | **(18)** ✗ |
| **(5)** ✗ | **(12)** ✗ | **(19)** ✓ |
| **(6)** ✗ | **(13)** ✓ | **(20)** ✗ |
| **(7)** ✓ | **(14)** ✗ | |

*(1) assist<u>a</u>nce; (3) cer<u>ea</u>l; (4) chemica<u>l</u>s; (5) depend<u>ence</u>; (6) dis<u>gu</u>ise; (8) hesit<u>a</u>nt; (10) impersonal; (11) inca<u>pa</u>ble; (12) <u>i</u>nformal; (14) int<u>er</u>sects; (16) mour<u>n</u>ing; (17) nou<u>g</u>ht; (18) pou<u>t</u>; (20) seri<u>a</u>l*

### TEST 18.3

| | | |
|---|---|---|
| **(1)** ✗ | **(8)** ✗ | **(15)** ✗ |
| **(2)** ✓ | **(9)** ✓ | **(16)** ✗ |

(3) ✓    (10) ✓    (17) ✗
(4) ✓    (11) ✗    (18) ✗
(5) ✗    (12) ✗    (19) ✓
(6) ✓    (13) ✓    (20) ✗
(7) ✗    (14) ✓

*(1)* a*ss*ent; *(5)* de*c*ency; *(7)* fough*t*; *(8)* imm*i*grate; *(11)* indefin*i*te; *(12)* inhum*ane*; *(15)* inva*l*id; *(16)* l*e*nience; *(17)* mus*cle*; *(18)* princip*le*; *(20)* stati*one*ry

## TEST 18.4

(1) ✓    (9) ✗    (17) ✓
(2) ✓    (10) ✗    (18) ✗
(3) ✗    (11) ✓    (19) ✓
(4) ✗    (12) ✓    (20) ✓
(5) ✗    (13) ✓    (21) ✓
(6) ✓    (14) ✓    (22) ✗
(7) ✓    (15) ✗
(8) ✓    (16) ✗

*(3)* compet*e*nce; *(4)* di*ss*ent; *(5)* differ*e*nce; *(9)* imp*o*lite; *(10)* ined*ib*le; *(15)* nui*s*ance; *(16)* proce*e*d; *(18)* rea*c*quaint; *(22)* th*o*rough

## TEST 18.5

(1) ✗    (9) ✗    (17) ✓
(2) ✓    (10) ✓    (18) ✓
(3) ✗    (11) ✓    (19) ✓
(4) ✗    (12) ✗    (20) ✓
(5) ✓    (13) ✗    (21) ✗
(6) ✗    (14) ✓    (22) ✗
(7) ✗    (15) ✓
(8) ✓    (16) ✓

*(1)* appa*r*ent; *(3)* c*o*logne; *(4)* caugh*t*; *(6)* fa*sc*inated; *(7)* hind*r*ance; *(9)* imp*r*actical; *(12)* li*c*ence; *(13)* med*dle*; *(21)* w*h*ether; *(22)* wrin*k*led

## TEST 18.6

(1) ✓    (9) ✗    (17) ✓
(2) ✓    (10) ✓    (18) ✓

(3) ✗    (11) ✗    (19) ✓
(4) ✓    (12) ✗    (20) ✓
(5) ✗    (13) ✓    (21) ✗
(6) ✓    (14) ✓    (22) ✗
(7) ✗    (15) ✗
(8) ✓    (16) ✓

*(3)* cu*rr*ant; *(5)* de*bt*; *(7)* hi*cc*ough; *(9)* imm*o*bile; *(11)* inse*pa*rable; *(12)* interlib*r*ary; *(15)* persist*e*nt; *(21)* solem*n*ly; *(22)* *w*rought

## TEST 18.7

(1) ✗    (9) ✗    (17) ✓
(2) ✓    (10) ✗    (18) ✗
(3) ✗    (11) ✗    (19) ✗
(4) ✗    (12) ✓    (20) ✗
(5) ✗    (13) ✓    (21) ✓
(6) ✓    (14) ✓    (22) ✓
(7) ✗    (15) ✓
(8) ✓    (16) ✗

*(1)* assist*a*nt; *(3)* compl*e*ments; *(4)* cough; *(5)* depend*e*ncy; *(7)* impai*r*ed; *(9)* ina*cc*urate; *(10)* increm*e*nt; *(11)* observ*a*nce; *(16)* rhym*e*s; *(18)* sough*t*; *(19)* this*tle*; *(20)* though*t*

## TEST 18.8

(1) ✗    (9) ✗    (17) ✗
(2) ✓    (10) ✓    (18) ✓
(3) ✓    (11) ✓    (19) ✓
(4) ✓    (12) ✗    (20) ✓
(5) ✗    (13) ✓    (21) ✗
(6) ✗    (14) ✓    (22) ✗
(7) ✓    (15) ✗
(8) ✓    (16) ✗

*(1)* a*l*tar; *(4)* defi*a*nt; *(5)* endur*a*nce; *(6)* f*r*aught; *(9)* insu*ff*icient; *(12)* negli*ge*nt; *(15)* rec*ei*pt; *(16)* rus*tl*ing; *(17)* substan*c*e; *(21)* wre*c*k; *(22)* vehi*cle*s

## TEST 18.9

(1) ✓    (9) ✓    (17) ✓
(2) ✓    (10) ✗    (18) ✗
(3) ✗    (11) ✗    (19) ✓
(4) ✓    (12) ✓    (20) ✗
(5) ✗    (13) ✓    (21) ✗
(6) ✓    (14) ✗    (22) ✓
(7) ✓    (15) ✓
(8) ✓    (16) ✓

*(3)* correspond*e*nt; *(5)* fu*r*ther; *(10)* malevol*e*nt; *(14)* re*ge*nerate; *(18)* thro*a*t; *(20)* toler*a*nce; *(21)* *w*eather

## TEST 18.10

(1) ✓    (9) ✓    (17) ✗
(2) ✗    (10) ✓    (18) ✗
(3) ✓    (11) ✓    (19) ✓
(4) ✗    (12) ✓    (20) ✓
(5) ✗    (13) ✗    (21) ✗
(6) ✗    (14) ✗    (22) ✗
(7) ✓    (15) ✓
(8) ✗    (16) ✓

*(2)* archa*e*ologist; *(4)* compliment; *(5)* coher*e*nt; *(6)* des*c*ent; *(8)* effici*e*ncy; *(13)* imp*e*rtinent; *(14)* inad*e*quate; *(17)* li*c*ense; *(18)* prin*c*iple; *(21)* suffici*e*ncy; *(22)* throug*h*out

## TEST 18.11

(1) ✗    (9) ✓    (17) ✗
(2) ✗    (10) ✗    (18) ✗
(3) ✓    (11) ✗    (19) ✓
(4) ✓    (12) ✓    (20) ✗
(5) ✗    (13) ✓    (21) ✗
(6) ✓    (14) ✓    (22) ✓
(7) ✓    (15) ✗
(8) ✗    (16) ✗

*(1)* a*l*oud; *(2)* brida*l*; *(5)* catac*o*mbs; *(8)* expect*a*nt; *(10)* immov*a*ble; *(11)* impre*c*ise; *(15)* med*dle*; *(16)* observ*a*nt; *(17)* pre*ce*de; *(18)* prophe*t*; *(20)* recu*r*;

*(21)* surveill*a*nce

| | | |
|---|---|---|
| **(1)** ✗ | **(9)** ✗ | **(17)** ✗ |
| **(2)** ✗ | **(10)** ✗ | **(18)** ✗ |
| **(3)** ✗ | **(11)** ✗ | **(19)** ✗ |
| **(4)** ✗ | **(12)** ✓ | **(20)** ✓ |
| **(5)** ✓ | **(13)** ✓ | **(21)** ✗ |
| **(6)** ✗ | **(14)** ✗ | **(22)** ✓ |
| **(7)** ✗ | **(15)** ✗ | |
| **(8)** ✓ | **(16)** ✓ | |

*(1)* assu*r*ances; *(2)* b*o*rough; *(3)* correspond*e*nce; *(4)* campai*g*ning; *(6)* eloquen*c*e; *(7)* fu*r*lough; *(9)* implaus*i*ble; *(10)* im*p*rudent; *(11)* indestruc*ti*ble; *(14)* *k*napsack; *(15)* lighte*n*ing; *(17)* p*n*eumonia; *(18)* resil*i*ence; *(19)* recip*i*ent; *(21)* su*cc*umbed

## UNIT 19

**(1)** super (supermarket)
**(2)** sub (subcommittee)
**(3)** anti (antiseptic)
**(4)** sub (subcategories)
**(5)** super (superstars)
**(6)** auto (autograph)
**(7)** sub (subconscious)
**(8)** anti (anticlimax)
**(9)** sub (submarine)
**(10)** auto (autobiographies)

**(11)** anticlockwise
**(12)** supernatural
**(13)** subtitle
**(14)** superhuman
**(15)** subtract
**(16)** anti-theft OR antitheft
**(17)** superman
**(18)** submerged
**(19)** automobiles
**(20)** superglue
**(21)** antibiotic
**(22)** superimposed
**(23)** subdivided
**(24)** Subway
**(25)** subheading
**(26)** supercomputers
**(27)** subeditor

## UNIT 20

**(1)** girls
**(2)** knaves
**(3)** tomatoes
**(4)** celebrations
**(5)** women
**(6)** mice
**(7)** ibises
**(8)** anniversaries
**(9)** feet
**(10)** men
**(11)** sheep
**(12)** privileges
**(13)** rhythms
**(14)** oxen
**(15)** igloos
**(16)** children
**(17)** teeth
**(18)** geese
**(19)** distilleries
**(20)** attendees
**(21)** foxes
**(22)** these
**(23)** miniatures
**(24)** wives
**(25)** cacti OR cactuses
**(26)** liabilities
**(27)** lice
**(28)** volcanoes OR volcanos
**(29)** allegories
**(30)** loaves
**(31)** crises
**(32)** deer
**(33)** those
**(34)** phenomena

**(35)** children's
**(36)** soldiers'
**(37)** fishes
**(38)** glasses
**(39)** shoes'
**(40)** controversies
**(41)** scarves
**(42)** amateurs'
**(43)** firemen's
**(44)** cookies
**(45)** radios'
**(46)** People's
**(47)** Cliffs
**(48)** fungi
**(49)** avocados
**(50)** quizzes'
**(51)** oases
**(52)** puppies'
**(53)** series
**(54)** hippopotamuses

## UNIT 21

**(1)** beginner
**(2)** gardener
**(3)** communicator
**(4)** forgotten
**(5)** limitation
**(6)** equipped
**(7)** sunburnt OR sunburned
**(8)** shipping
**(9)** occurring
**(10)** nagging
**(11)** preparations
**(12)** acquitted
**(13)** engineer
**(14)** bargaining
**(15)** overpopulation
**(16)** babysitter
**(17)** shouldered
**(18)** strummed
**(19)** carrier

**(20)** C. CCOMMODATE ⇨ accommodated
**(21)** A. NSURIN ⇨ insuring
**(22)** D. ORMATTE ⇨ formatted
**(23)** C. MITTIN ⇨ emitting
**(24)** B. NFOCUSE ⇨ unfocused
**(25)** D. MBARRASSMEN ⇨ embarrassment
**(26)** B. EVELOPMEN ⇨ development
**(27)** D. AVESDROPPE ⇨ eavesdropper
**(28)** A. RONOUNCE ⇨ pronounced
**(29)** C. XAGGERATE ⇨ exaggerated

## UNIT 22

**(1)** deferral ✓
confe*r*rence ✗ ⇨ confe*r*ence
dif*f*rence ✗ ⇨ diff*e*rence
suffe*rr*ed ✗ ⇨ suffe*r*ed
**(2)** offered ✓
infe*r*ed ✗ ⇨ infe*rr*ed
sur*ff*ing ✗ ⇨ sur*f*ing
refe*r*ance ✗ ⇨ refe*r*ence
**(3)** preference ✓

referal ✗ ⇨ referral
differring ✗ ⇨ differing
confered ✗ ⇨ conferred
**(4)** refereed ✓
referrendum ✗ ⇨ referendum
transferance ✗ ⇨ transference
pilferring ✗ ⇨ pilfering

**(5)** B. deference
**(6)** A. conferring
**(7)** C. deferred
**(8)** D. offering
**(9)** A. inference
**(10)** B. pilfered
**(11)** C. suffering
**(12)** A. surfer
**(13)** D. preferred
**(14)** B. interfere

## UNIT 23

**(1)** music + cian ⇨ musician
**(2)** commit + ssion ⇨ commission
**(3)** decide + sion ⇨ decision
**(4)** educate + tion ⇨ education
**(5)** discuss + ssion ⇨ discussion
**(6)** adopt + tion ⇨ adoption
**(7)** include + sion ⇨ inclusion
**(8)** operate + tion ⇨ operation
**(9)** suggest + tion ⇨ suggestion
**(10)** electric + cian ⇨ electrician
**(11)** predict + tion ⇨ prediction
**(12)** express + ssion ⇨ expression
**(13)** submit + ssion ⇨ submission
**(14)** elect + tion ⇨ election
**(15)** promote + tion ⇨ promotion
**(16)** divide + sion ⇨ division
**(17)** comprehend + sion ⇨ comprehension
**(18)** attend + tion ⇨ attention
**(19)** compress + ssion ⇨ compression
**(20)** insert + tion ⇨ insertion
**(21)** diffuse + sion ⇨ diffusion
**(22)** omit + ssion ⇨ omission
**(23)** distort + tion ⇨ distortion
**(24)** suspend + sion ⇨ suspension
**(25)** profess + ssion ⇨ profession
**(26)** graduate + tion ⇨

graduation
**(27)** project + tion ⇨ projection
**(28)** devote + tion ⇨ devotion
**(29)** contract + tion ⇨ contraction
**(30)** clinic + cian ⇨ clinician
**(31)** prevent + tion ⇨ prevention
**(32)** transmit + ssion ⇨ transmission

**(33)** illustration
**(34)** optician
**(35)** impression
**(36)** pollution
**(37)** admission
**(38)** confusion
**(39)** confession
**(40)** indication
**(41)** exception
**(42)** permission
**(43)** exhaustion
**(44)** explosion
**(45)** statistician
**(46)** intention
**(47)** accommodation
**(48)** digestion
**(49)** intrusion
**(50)** desertion
**(51)** emission

## UNIT 24

### TEST 24.1

| | | |
|---|---|---|
| **(1)** ✓ | **(8)** ✗ | **(15)** ✓ |
| **(2)** ✓ | **(9)** ✗ | **(16)** ✓ |
| **(3)** ✓ | **(10)** ✓ | **(17)** ✗ |
| **(4)** ✓ | **(11)** ✓ | **(18)** ✗ |
| **(5)** ✓ | **(12)** ✓ | **(19)** ✓ |
| **(6)** ✗ | **(13)** ✓ | **(20)** ✗ |
| **(7)** ✓ | **(14)** ✗ | |

**(6)** categories; **(8)** committee; **(9)** difference; **(14)** igloo; **(17)** occur; **(18)** preparations; **(20)** rhythms

### TEST 24.2

| | | |
|---|---|---|
| **(1)** ✗ | **(8)** ✓ | **(15)** ✓ |
| **(2)** ✓ | **(9)** ✗ | **(16)** ✗ |
| **(3)** ✓ | **(10)** ✓ | **(17)** ✗ |
| **(4)** ✓ | **(11)** ✗ | **(18)** ✗ |
| **(5)** ✗ | **(12)** ✓ | **(19)** ✗ |
| **(6)** ✓ | **(13)** ✗ | **(20)** ✗ |
| **(7)** ✓ | **(14)** ✓ | |

**(1)** autobiographies; **(5)** conference; **(9)** decision; **(11)** fishes'; **(13)** goose's; **(16)** ox; **(17)** privilege; **(18)** people's; **(19)** referral; **(20)** suffering

### TEST 24.3

| | | |
|---|---|---|
| **(1)** ✗ | **(8)** ✗ | **(15)** ✓ |
| **(2)** ✗ | **(9)** ✗ | **(16)** ✓ |
| **(3)** ✓ | **(10)** ✗ | **(17)** ✗ |
| **(4)** ✓ | **(11)** ✓ | **(18)** ✗ |
| **(5)** ✗ | **(12)** ✗ | **(19)** ✗ |
| **(6)** ✗ | **(13)** ✓ | **(20)** ✓ |
| **(7)** ✗ | **(14)** ✓ | |

**(1)** acquit; **(2)** allegory; **(5)** communicate; **(6)** contraction; **(7)** deferred; **(8)** distillery; **(9)** development; **(10)** election; **(12)** glasses; **(17)** pilfered; **(18)** phenomenon; **(19)** sunburned

### TEST 24.4

| | | |
|---|---|---|
| **(1)** ✗ | **(9)** ✗ | **(17)** ✓ |
| **(2)** ✓ | **(10)** ✗ | **(18)** ✗ |
| **(3)** ✗ | **(11)** ✓ | **(19)** ✗ |
| **(4)** ✓ | **(12)** ✓ | **(20)** ✓ |
| **(5)** ✓ | **(13)** ✗ | **(21)** ✓ |
| **(6)** ✗ | **(14)** ✗ | **(22)** ✗ |
| **(7)** ✓ | **(15)** ✗ | |
| **(8)** ✓ | **(16)** ✗ | |

**(1)** accommodated; **(3)** confusion; **(6)** discussion; **(9)** geese; **(10)** illustration; **(13)** miniature; **(14)** offered; **(15)** pollution; **(16)** profession; **(18)** suspension; **(19)** suggestion; **(22)** tomato

### TEST 24.5

| | | |
|---|---|---|
| **(1)** ✗ | **(9)** ✗ | **(17)** ✓ |
| **(2)** ✓ | **(10)** ✓ | **(18)** ✓ |
| **(3)** ✗ | **(11)** ✗ | **(19)** ✗ |

(4) × (12) × (20) ✓
(5) ✓ (13) ✓ (21) ✓
(6) × (14) × (22) ✓
(7) ✓ (15) ×
(8) ✓ (16) ×

(1) anniversaries; (3) conferred; (4) children's; (6) deference; (9) igloos; (11) overpopulate; (12) omission; (14) preference; (15) preferred; (16) reference; (19) shipping

## TEST 24.6

(1) ✓ (9) ✓ (17) ✓
(2) × (10) ✓ (18) ×
(3) ✓ (11) ✓ (19) ✓
(4) × (12) × (20) ✓
(5) × (13) ✓ (21) ✓
(6) ✓ (14) × (22) ×
(7) ✓ (15) ✓
(8) × (16) ✓

(2) child's; (4) crises; (5) deer; (8) interfere; (12) pronounced; (14) series; (18) subcommittee; (22) unfocused

## TEST 24.7

(1) ✓ (9) ✓ (17) ✓
(2) ✓ (10) × (18) ×
(3) ✓ (11) ✓ (19) ✓
(4) ✓ (12) × (20) ✓
(5) × (13) ✓ (21) ×
(6) × (14) ✓ (22) ✓
(7) × (15) ×
(8) ✓ (16) ×

(5) distortion; (6) expression; (7) gardener; (10) operation; (12) promotion; (15) subconscious; (16) subcategories; (18) septic; (21) whose

## TEST 24.8

(1) × (9) ✓ (17) ✓
(2) × (10) ✓ (18) ✓

(3) × (11) × (19) ×
(4) × (12) ✓ (20) ✓
(5) ✓ (13) ✓ (21) ×
(6) × (14) ✓ (22) ✓
(7) ✓ (15) ×
(8) ✓ (16) ✓

(1) amateurs; (2) beginner; (3) cliffs; (4) compression; (5) distilleries; (6) exaggerated; (11) prevention; (15) subeditor; (19) thief; (21) transmission

## TEST 24.9

(1) ✓ (9) ✓ (17) ×
(2) ✓ (10) × (18) ×
(3) × (11) ✓ (19) ✓
(4) × (12) ✓ (20) ✓
(5) × (13) ✓ (21) ✓
(6) ✓ (14) ✓ (22) ✓
(7) × (15) ✓
(8) ✓ (16) ×

(3) communicator; (4) controversies; (5) differing; (7) emitting; (10) feet; (12) inferred; (16) puppies'; (17) referendum; (18) suffered

## TEST 24.10

(1) × (9) × (17) ✓
(2) ✓ (10) × (18) ×
(3) × (11) ✓ (19) ×
(4) ✓ (12) × (20) ✓
(5) ✓ (13) ✓ (21) ✓
(6) × (14) ✓ (22) ✓
(7) ✓ (15) ×
(8) × (16) ×

(1) allegories; (3) avocados; (6) crisis; (8) deferral; (9) exception; (10) forgotten; (12) ibises; (15) offering; (16) optician; (18) pilfering; (19) strummed

## TEST 24.11

(1) ✓ (9) × (17) ✓

(2) ✓ (10) ✓ (18) ×
(3) × (11) ✓ (19) ✓
(4) ✓ (12) × (20) ✓
(5) ✓ (13) ✓ (21) ×
(6) × (14) ✓ (22) ×
(7) × (15) ×
(8) ✓ (16) ×

(3) bargaining; (6) desertion; (7) exhaustion; (9) firemen's; (12) liabilities; (15) oases; (16) rhythm; (18) sheep; (21) tomatoes; (22) volcanoes

## TEST 24.12

(1) ✓ (9) ✓ (17) ×
(2) × (10) × (18) ✓
(3) × (11) ✓ (19) ×
(4) × (12) × (20) ×
(5) × (13) ✓ (21) ✓
(6) × (14) ✓ (22) ×
(7) ✓ (15) ✓
(8) × (16) ✓

(2) acquitted; (3) antiseptic; (4) conferring; (6) diffusion; (8) eavesdropper; (10) formatted; (12) inference; (17) statistician; (19) swot; (20) transference; (22) wives'

## UNIT 25

(1) interested; superb
(2) antic; comet
(3) discos; preen
(4) counter; relative
(5) inner; mister
(6) comma; coining
(7) proudly; reedy
(8) imagine; prowler
(9) antique; unit
(10) comely; condor
(11) under; profiterole
(12) interred; prodigy
(13) mistletoe; interim
(14) intern; properly
(15) conical; probing

(16) imperceptible

**(17)** <u>un</u>professional
**(18)** <u>in</u>accessible
**(19)** <u>dis</u>advantage
**(20)** <u>un</u>compromising
**(21)** <u>in</u>considerate
**(22)** <u>un</u>characteristic
**(23)** <u>ir</u>replaceable
**(24)** <u>dis</u>belief
**(25)** <u>un</u>bearable
**(26)** <u>un</u>insured
**(27)** <u>in</u>animate
**(28)** <u>in</u>eligible
**(29)** <u>ir</u>reconcilable
**(30)** <u>dis</u>regarded
**(31)** <u>un</u>patriotic
**(32)** <u>in</u>appropriate
**(33)** <u>un</u>remarkable
**(34)** <u>in</u>effective

## UNIT 26

**(1) - (10)** *The 10 incorrectly spelt words and their correct spellings are as follows:*
disturb<u>e</u>nce ⇨ disturb<u>a</u>nce
<u>in</u>acknowledged ⇨ <u>un</u>acknowledged
improb<u>i</u>bly ⇨ improb<u>a</u>bly
<u>un</u>relevance ⇨ <u>ir</u>relevance
<u>dis</u>diagnose ⇨ <u>mis</u>diagnose
<u>mis</u>approvingly ⇨ <u>dis</u>approvingly
<u>in</u>drinkable ⇨ <u>un</u>drinkable
<u>ree</u>valuation ⇨ <u>re-e</u>valuation
<u>un</u>admissable ⇨ <u>in</u>admissible
<u>in</u>personated ⇨ <u>im</u>personated

**(11)** irreparable
**(12)** indefinable OR undefinable
**(13)** inexperience
**(14)** encouragement
**(15)** proficiency
**(16)** irreverent
**(17)** misgovernment
**(18)** disagreement
**(19)** inconsistent OR inconsistency
**(20)** disrespectful
**(21)** reassurance
**(22)** imprudence
**(23)** unemployment
**(24)** irretrievable

**(25)** <u>jab</u> + <u>ed</u> ⇨ jabbed
**(26)** <u>president</u> + <u>tial</u> ⇨

presidential
**(27)** <u>induce</u> + <u>ible</u> ⇨ inducible
**(28)** <u>guide</u> + <u>ance</u> ⇨ guidance
**(29)** <u>differ</u> + <u>ed</u> ⇨ differed
**(30)** <u>irritate</u> + <u>tion</u> ⇨ irritation
**(31)** <u>urge</u> + <u>ency</u> ⇨ urgency
**(32)** <u>obsess</u> + <u>ssion</u> ⇨ obsession
**(33)** <u>chisel</u> + <u>ing</u> ⇨ chiselling
**(34)** <u>comply</u> + <u>ant</u> ⇨ compliant
**(35)** <u>invent</u> + <u>tion</u> ⇨ invention
**(36)** <u>hysterical</u> + <u>ly</u> ⇨ hysterically
OR <u>hysteric</u> + <u>ally</u> ⇨ hysterically
**(37)** <u>persuade</u> + <u>sion</u> ⇨
persuasion
**(38)** <u>rhetoric</u> + <u>cian</u> ⇨
rhetorician
**(39)** <u>able</u> + <u>ly</u> ⇨ ably
**(40)** <u>plod</u> + <u>er</u> ⇨ plodder
**(41)** <u>transfer</u> + <u>ing</u> ⇨ transferring
**(42)** <u>erode</u> + <u>sion</u> ⇨ erosion
**(43)** <u>eerie</u> + <u>ly</u> ⇨ eerily
**(44)** <u>trek</u> + <u>ed</u> ⇨ trekked
**(45)** <u>classify</u> + <u>able</u> ⇨ classifiable
**(46)** <u>idealistic</u> + <u>ally</u> ⇨
idealistically
**(47)** <u>conscience</u> + <u>tious</u> ⇨
conscientious
**(48)** <u>transgress</u> + <u>ssion</u> ⇨
transgression
**(49)** <u>absorb</u> + <u>ent</u> ⇨ absorbent
**(50)** <u>forensic</u> + <u>ally</u> ⇨ forensically
**(51)** <u>consequent</u> + <u>tial</u> ⇨
consequential
**(52)** <u>occupy</u> + <u>ancy</u> ⇨ occupancy
**(53)** <u>cohere</u> + <u>ence</u> ⇨ coherence
**(54)** <u>flog</u> + <u>ing</u> ⇨ flogging
**(55)** <u>complete</u> + <u>tion</u> ⇨
completion
**(56)** <u>success</u> + <u>ssion</u> ⇨
succession

## UNIT 27

**(1)** ours
**(2)** boss
**(3)** thief
**(4)** chiefs
**(5)** complex
**(6)** echoes
**(7)** bookworm
**(8)** theirs
**(9)** anchovy
**(10)** alleys
**(11)** mattress

**(12)** puffs
**(13)** rhinoceroses OR rhinoceros
**(14)** myself
**(15)** handkerchiefs
**(16)** advice
**(17)** giraffes
**(18)** moose
**(19)** barracks
**(20)** lampshade
**(21)** matchstick
**(22)** commandos OR commandoes
**(23)** index
**(24)** beliefs
**(25)** ally
**(26)** torpedoes
**(27)** yours
**(28)** confectioneries
**(29)** offspring
**(30)** axe
**(31)** zeros
**(32)** archipelagos OR archipelagoes

**(33)** bis<u>ons</u> ✗ ⇨ bis<u>on</u>
**(34)** information<u>s</u> ✗ ⇨ information<u>n</u>
**(35)** cargo<u>es'</u> ✗ ⇨ cargo<u>es</u> OR cargos
**(36)** roof<u>'s</u> ✗ ⇨ roof<u>s</u>
**(37)** bookshel<u>fs</u> ✗ ⇨ bookshel<u>ves</u>
**(38)** oboes<u>'s</u> ✗ ⇨ oboes<u>'</u>
**(39)** potat<u>os</u> ✗ ⇨ potat<u>oes</u>
**(40)** waltz<u>es'</u> ✗ ⇨ waltz<u>es</u>
**(41)** dragons<u>'s</u> ✗ ⇨ dragons<u>'</u>
**(42)** Mosquit<u>os</u> ✗ ⇨ Mosquit<u>oes'</u> OR Mosquitos' OR Mosquito
**(43)** yours<u>'</u> ✗ ⇨ yours<u>s</u>
**(44)** hoax<u>'s</u> ✗ ⇨ hoax<u>es</u>

## UNIT 28

**(1)** d r <u>a</u> k <u>e</u>
**(2)** d <u>u</u> c k
**(3)** r <u>o</u> <u>o</u> s t <u>e</u> r
**(4)** h <u>e</u> n
**(5)** g <u>a</u> n <u>d</u> <u>e</u> r
**(6)** g <u>o</u> <u>o</u> s <u>e</u>
**(7)** b <u>o</u> a r
**(8)** s <u>o</u> w
**(9)** r <u>a</u> m
**(10)** e w <u>e</u>
**(11)** t <u>o</u> m
**(12)** t <u>i</u> g <u>r</u> <u>e</u> <u>s</u> <u>s</u>

(13) d r o n e
(14) s t a g
(15) v i x e n
(16) p e a h e n
(17) b u l l
(18) c o w

(19) duchess
(20) bridegroom OR groom
(21) heiress
(22) lord
(23) shepherd
(24) daughter
(25) waiter
(26) sister
(27) abbess
(28) maidservant
(29) hero
(30) stewardess
(31) Mrs
(32) lass
(33) prince
(34) master
(35) countess
(36) headmistress
(37) goddess
(38) empress
(39) sir
(40) actress
(41) sire
(42) sultana
(43) wizard OR warlock
(44) widower
(45) nun
(46) spinster
(47) aunt
(48) marchioness
(49) fiancé
(50) billy goat

(1) pact
(2) imminent
(3) we're
(4) arms
(5) bazaar
(6) mettle
(7) oral
(8) foreword
(9) quarts
(10) borne
(11) wreak
(12) swot

(13) coarse
(14) troop
(15) stake
(16) duel
(17) sought
(18) naval
(19) cast
(20) where
(21) guerrilla
(22) suite
(23) tolled
(24) hail
(25) whine
(26) mowed
(27) lava
(28) gilt
(29) their
(30) lone
(31) counsel
(32) borders
(33) horde
(34) lessen
(35) ads
(36) Fates
(37) laps
(38) hangers
(39) peel
(40) whet
(41) storey

**TEST 30.1**

| | | |
|---|---|---|
| (1) × | (8) ✓ | (15) × |
| (2) × | (9) × | (16) × |
| (3) × | (10) ✓ | (17) ✓ |
| (4) × | (11) × | (18) ✓ |
| (5) ✓ | (12) ✓ | (19) × |
| (6) ✓ | (13) × | (20) ✓ |
| (7) × | (14) × | |

*(1)* abbot; *(2)* bizarre; *(3)* compliant; *(4)* cargoes; *(7)* empress; *(9)* forward; *(11)* headmaster; *(13)* imminent; *(14)* increase *(15)* inconsistent; *(16)* indices; *(19)* offspring

**TEST 30.2**

| | | |
|---|---|---|
| (1) ✓ | (8) × | (15) ✓ |
| (2) ✓ | (9) ✓ | (16) ✓ |
| (3) × | (10) ✓ | (17) × |
| (4) × | (11) × | (18) ✓ |
| (5) × | (12) ✓ | (19) × |
| (6) × | (13) ✓ | (20) × |
| (7) ✓ | (14) × | |

*(3)* calypsos; *(4)* disagreement; *(5)* discolour; *(6)* drone; *(8)* handkerchiefs; *(11)* information; *(14)* llama; *(17)* aural; *(19)* quarts; *(20)* reallocated

**TEST 30.3**

| | | |
|---|---|---|
| (1) ✓ | (8) ✓ | (15) ✓ |
| (2) ✓ | (9) × | (16) ✓ |
| (3) ✓ | (10) × | (17) × |
| (4) × | (11) × | (18) ✓ |
| (5) ✓ | (12) ✓ | (19) ✓ |
| (6) ✓ | (13) ✓ | (20) × |
| (7) × | (14) × | |

*(4)* consequential; *(7)* duchess; *(9)* heiress; *(10)* ill-advised; *(11)* imperceptible; *(14)* marquis; *(17)* occupancy; *(20)* redoubling

**TEST 30.4**

| | | |
|---|---|---|
| (1) × | (9) ✓ | (17) × |
| (2) ✓ | (10) × | (18) ✓ |
| (3) × | (11) × | (19) × |
| (4) × | (12) ✓ | (20) ✓ |
| (5) ✓ | (13) ✓ | (21) × |
| (6) ✓ | (14) ✓ | (22) ✓ |
| (7) × | (15) ✓ | |
| (8) × | (16) ✓ | |

*(1)* ably; *(3)* completion; *(4)* commandoes; *(7)* eerily; *(8)* gorilla; *(10)* improper; *(11)* inaccessible; *(17)* reassurance; *(19)* barracks; *(21)* their

**TEST 30.5**

| | | |
|---|---|---|
| (1) ✓ | (9) × | (17) ✓ |
| (2) ✓ | (10) ✓ | (18) × |
| (3) × | (11) × | (19) ✓ |

(4) ✓ (12) × (20) ✓
(5) ✓ (13) ✓ (21) ×
(6) × (14) × (22) ✓
(7) × (15) ✓
(8) ✓ (16) ✓

(3) chiselling; (6) echoes; (7) fiancée; (9) inadmissible; (11) irreconcilable; (12) luxuries; (14) navel; (18) spinster; (21) uninsured

## TEST 30.6

(1) ✓ (9) ✓ (17) ✓
(2) × (10) ✓ (18) ✓
(3) ✓ (11) × (19) ✓
(4) ✓ (12) ✓ (20) ✓
(5) × (13) ✓ (21) ×
(6) ✓ (14) × (22) ×
(7) ✓ (15) ×
(8) × (16) ×

(2) council; (5) disapprovingly; (8) impersonated; (11) irredeemable; (14) ourselves; (15) profess; (16) re-evaluation; (21) unprofessional; (22) urgency

## TEST 30.7

(1) × (9) ✓ (17) ✓
(2) ✓ (10) × (18) ×
(3) ✓ (11) × (19) ×
(4) ✓ (12) ✓ (20) ✓
(5) ✓ (13) ✓ (21) ×
(6) ✓ (14) ✓ (22) ✓
(7) ✓ (15) ×
(8) ✓ (16) ✓

(1) anchovies; (10) irrelevance; (11) irreverent; (15) rhythms; (18) troupe; (19) uninterested; (21) waitress

## TEST 30.8

(1) ✓ (9) × (17) ×
(2) ✓ (10) × (18) ×
(3) ✓ (11) × (19) ✓
(4) ✓ (12) ✓ (20) ✓
(5) ✓ (13) ✓ (21) ×
(6) ✓ (14) × (22) ✓
(7) × (15) ✓
(8) ✓ (16) ✓

(7) goddess; (9) imprisonment; (10) inappropriate; (11) inconsistency; (14) obsession; (17) they're; (18) thieves; (21) unemployment

## TEST 30.9

(1) × (9) × (17) ×
(2) ✓ (10) × (18) ✓
(3) ✓ (11) ✓ (19) ✓
(4) × (12) × (20) ✓
(5) ✓ (13) ✓ (21) ✓
(6) ✓ (14) × (22) ✓
(7) × (15) ✓
(8) × (16) ×

(1) absorbent; (4) dissatisfied; (7) extracurricular; (8) forward; (9) guidance; (10) encouragement; (12) irritation; (14) mouths; (16) suite; (17) steward

## TEST 30.10

(1) ✓ (9) × (17) ×
(2) ✓ (10) × (18) ✓
(3) ✓ (11) × (19) ×
(4) × (12) × (20) ×
(5) ✓ (13) ✓ (21) ×
(6) ✓ (14) ✓ (22) ✓
(7) × (15) ×
(8) ✓ (16) ×

(4) bosses; (7) disturbance; (9) hoard; (10) ineligible; (11) insignificance; (12) irreplaceable; (15) misremembered; (16) perceptible; (17) rhinoceroses; (19) trekked; (20) unremarkably; (21) unpatriotic

## TEST 30.11

(1) × (9) ✓ (17) ✓
(2) ✓ (10) × (18) ×
(3) × (11) × (19) ×
(4) ✓ (12) ✓ (20) ×
(5) × (13) ✓ (21) ×
(6) × (14) ✓ (22) ×
(7) ✓ (15) ×
(8) ✓ (16) ×

(1) autonomous; (3) coherence; (5) disrespectful; (6) flogging; (10) imprudence; (11) mosquito; (15) theirs; (16) transferring; (18) ungrammatical; (19) unrepentant; (20) unresolvable; (21) waltzes; (22) wreak

## TEST 30.12

(1) ✓ (9) × (17) ×
(2) × (10) ✓ (18) ✓
(3) × (11) ✓ (19) ✓
(4) ✓ (12) ✓ (20) ×
(5) ✓ (13) × (21) ✓
(6) × (14) × (22) ×
(7) × (15) ×
(8) × (16) ✓

(2) bachelor; (3) confectionery; (6) disoriented; (7) erosion; (8) extraterrestrial; (9) fêtes; (13) proficiency; (14) rhetorician; (15) shepherdess; (17) supersede; (20) uncompromising; (22) zeros

# WORDS IN FOCUS

UNIT 1

tomorrow
forty
criticises
identity
variety
probably
awkward
occupied
developing
familiar
relevant
amateur
harassed
definite
twelfth
Wednesday
attached
category
bruised
wonderful

accident
occasion
cemetery
parliament
recognise
dictionary
sincere
determined
explanation
signature
queue
embarrass
programme
community
competition
guarantee
vehicle
physical
correspond
eight
neighbour
accompany
secretary

yacht
available

necessary
government
pronunciation
temperature
according
vegetable
individual
restaurant
excellent

disappear
strength
build
medicine
exercise
group
circle
straight
address
calendar
separate
ordinary
fruit
imagine
particular
height
learn
recent
natural
favourite
often
quarter
actually
through
thorough
strange
surprise
popular
remember
breathe
consider
decide
certain
perhaps
purpose
century
interest
important
therefore
sentence
grammar

desperate
earth

controversy
determination
interrupted
recommend
curiosity
sacrifice
prejudice
February
desperately
committee
accompaniment
argument
eighth
languages
occurrences
communication
environment
actual
sincerity

ancient
system
diligent
aggressive
shoulder
centre
knowledge
convenience
rhythm
average
complete
accidentally
especially
peculiar
continue
existence
opportunity
detached
describe
equipment
frequently
sincerely
possession
minute
experiment
experience
expertise
develop
soldier
possible
parallel

history
guard
naughty
material
forwards
mention
bicycle
appear
library
extreme
suppose
rhyme
length
thought

woman
breath
questions
difficult
increase
busy
arrive
early
guide
promised
enough
pressure
notice
opposite
regular
occasionally
positions
though

UNIT 2

reincarnation
coincide
anti-inflammatory
co-operation
reimburse
collaborate
de-emphasise
deduce
antihero
anti-hero
re-employ
recurring
semicircle
reduce
collision
redeem

re-enter

co-ordination
semiautomatic
semi-automatic
redesigned
microbiologist
de-escalate
re-editing
antibodies
co-organisers
semicolon
demoted
re-examining
antisocial
re-elected
co-operate
micro-organism

## UNIT 3

friend
leisure
anxiety
convenient
reign
freight
foreign
eiderdown
impatient
briefcase
weight
neighbourhood
yield
reindeer
sovereign
hygiene
gondolier

quiet
relieved
seized
besieged
counterfeit
eighteenth
unveiling
ingredient
reins
lenient
grieved
died
brigadier
lieutenant
pieces
chandelier
believe

aliens
niece
disobedient
poltergeist
weird
scientific
well-received
decaffeinated
beige

## UNIT 4

cautious
tiptoed
vicious
defenceless
sailor
precious
nutritious
unappetising
boring
repetitious
nonsense
fictitious
ambitious
monotonous
spacious
luxurious
voracious
atrocious

delicious
malicious
curious
famous
various
poisonous
anxious
suspicious
adventurous
superstitious
barbarous
hideous
mountainous
dangerous
perilous
humongous
conscious
hazardous
infamous
luscious
marvellous
tremendous
outrageous

jealous
precarious
precipitous
precocious
tedious
joyous
glamorous
gracious
infectious
anonymous
vigorous
treacherous
venomous
ridiculous
thunderous
herbivorous
fabulous
disastrous
pretentious
prosperous
rebellious
stupendous

## UNIT 5

essential
confidential
artificial
officials
provincial
special
residential
glacial
social
infomercials

superficial
financial
partial
commercial
potential
sequential
racial
palatial
crucial
influential
especial
martial
impartial
facial
unofficial
beneficial
judicial
substantial

## UNIT 7

courage
discourage
lead
mislead
relevant
irrelevant
behave
misbehave
possess
dispossess
print
misprint
address
misaddress
regular
irregular
obey
disobey
govern
misgovern
legal
illegal
count
discount
miscount
agree
disagree
guide
misguide
heard
misheard
appoint
disappoint
legible
illegible
rational
irrational
allow
disallow
regard
disregard
misregard
pose
dispose
fit
misfit
shaped
misshaped
arm
disarm
able
disable

align
misalign
conduct
misconduct
card
discard
grace
disgrace
honest
dishonest
handle
mishandle
label
mislabel

illiterate
disapproval
misspelled
misspelt
irresponsible
disappearance
misremember
dissatisfied
discontinuing
mistreatment
disadvantage
disagreeable
illogical
mistrustful
irresistible
disappointment
misapprehension
misdeed
irreversible
mislaid
disembarked
discourteous
misdirection
disassemble
discomfort
misinformation
disenchanted
misconception
dissimilarity
misapplied
disruption
misspeak
disorderly
misjudged
dismissal
illegitimate
disbelievingly

## UNIT 8

conceive
mischievous
conscience
species
ceiling
achievement
nuclei
societies
juiciest
concierge
piecemeal
receipts
glacier
financier
piercingly
deceivers
recipes
deficiency
omniscient
transceivers
conceitedness
unperceived

## UNIT 9

scheme
chorus
charity
anarchy
crypt
calypso
lyric
psyche
mascot
crescent
cascade
fiasco
cyanide
photosynthesis
syndicate
synonym
Achilles
bronchitis
enchilada
monarchy
symbol
rye
typical
symptom
martyr
sty
pyre

typhoon
obscene
adolescent
scimitar
crescendo
chided
urchins
archipelago
besmirched
gymkhana
gyroscope
hymn
gymnasium
hibiscus
escapade
fresco
fluorescent

asymmetrical
charismatic
schemes
isosceles
cyclists
orchestra
echoing
chrysanthemums
scenery
platypus
effervescent
architect
susceptible
sceptre
chameleon
tympani
character
scholar
hierarchical

chef
tongue
moustache
unique
machine
league
brochure
parachute
chalet
antique
colleagues
boutique
plague
chivalry
bouquet
chandelier

catalogue
pistachio
cheque

picturesque
consequence
quest
squeak
bewitch
challenge
archer
champagne
banquet
racquet
prequel
squelch
query
aqueduct
physique
queasy
orchid
chlorine
stomach
fuchsia
request
grotesque
squeeze
frequent
arachnid
chaperone
machete
chivalrous
technique
mosque
question
plaque
avalanche
crochet
crèche
archive
chic
chasm
chauffeur
charade
bequeath
equestrian
querulous
opaque

## UNIT 10

democratic
democratically
separate

separately
harsh
harshly
grave
gravely
begrudging
begrudgingly
literal
literally
flimsy
flimsily
magic
magically
naive
naively
persuasive
persuasively
complete
completely
abominable
abominably
ready
readily
historic
historically
ordinary
ordinarily
precise
precisely
cryptic
cryptically
hoarse
hoarsely
environment
environmentally

miserably
basically
immediately
cheerily
inexplicably
pompously
academically
temporarily
tangibly
elaborately

UNIT 11

prevent
preventable
envy
enviable
apply

applicable
mention
mentionable
adore
adorable
question
questionable
admit
admissible
reverse
reversible
like
likeable
answer
answerable
construct
constructable
constructible
imagine
imaginable
deny
deniable
attach
attachable
deduce
deducible
regret
regrettable
knowledge
knowledgeable
recommend
recommendable
programme
programmable
achieve
achievable
vary
variable
access
accessible
breathe
breathable
suggest
suggestible
collapse
collapsible
destruct
destructible
tolerate
tolerable
suppose
supposable
divide
divisible

consume
consumable
collect
collectible
appreciate
appreciable

conclusion
debatable
damage
considerably
suggestion
sensibly
comfortable
purchase
legible
impossible
reliable
changeable
forcible
persuadable
dependably
enjoyable
noticeably
understandable

UNIT 13

mature
immature
attentive
inattentive
correct
incorrect
balance
imbalance
advisable
inadvisable
mortal
immortal
patient
impatient
definite
indefinite
prudent
imprudent
famous
infamous
adequate
inadequate
practical
impractical
sufficient
insufficient

precise
imprecise
justice
injustice
valid
invalid
moral
immoral
edible
inedible
moveable
immoveable

interview
review
immigrate
indirect
redirect
innovate
renovate
implied
replied
retake
intake
rejected
injected
interjected
interplay
replay
infused
refused
intersects
insects
reformed
informed
imported
reported
reconnect
interconnect
impelled
repelled
reactive
inactive
intermediate
immediate
incur
recur
repaired
impaired
inclined
reclined

national
international

decorate
redecorate
prove
improve
humane
inhumane
accurate
inaccurate
act
react
interact
claim
reclaim
change
interchange
polite
impolite
acquaint
reacquaint
formal
informal
city
intercity
plant
implant
replant
library
interlibrary
fund
refund
consider
reconsider
destructible
indestructible
personal
impersonal
interpersonal
mission
remission
intermission
capable
incapable
dignity
indignity
boot
reboot
mobile
immobile
compatible
incompatible
twine
intertwine
generate
regenerate

separable
inseparable
plausible
implausible
material
immaterial
galactic
intergalactic
conclusive
inconclusive
pertinent
impertinent

UNIT 14

rough
tough
ruff
cough
doubt
drought
route
clout
foe
tow
dough
vow
trout
bought
wart
fraught
thorough
duller
cower
colour
trough
plough
bough
thou
ewe
true
through
rogue
thought
naught
draught
wrought
hour
flower
borough
sour
nought
caught
quart

chart
south
sought
sort
fort
fought
pout
taut
taught
throughout
nowt
gout
throat
bellow
furlough
sallow
allow
bout
ought
thwart
distraught
although
below
hiccough
woe

UNIT 15

doubts
muscle
island
biscuits
lamb
vehicles
business
solemnly
succumbed
thistle
cologne

fascinated
archaeologist
nuisance
queued
wrinkled
scent
wreck
rhymes
receipt
rustling
chemicals
guarantees
gnashed
pneumonia

disguise
debt
knapsack
campaigning
catacombs

UNIT 16

observe
observant
observance
differ
different
difference
hinder
hindrance
obey
obedient
obedience
hesitate
hesitant
hesitancy
hesitance
expect
expectant
expectancy
expectance
reside
resident
residence
residency
assist
assistant
assistance
correspond
correspondent
correspondence
suffice
sufficient
sufficiency
survey
surveillance
depend
dependant
dependent
dependence
dependency

increment
efficiency
innocent
substance
decency
tolerance

independent
confident
frequency
insistent
persistent
disobedience
assurances
negligent
recipient
eloquence
brilliance
defiant
endurance
resilience
component
coherent
competent
malevolent
lenience
sentences
inefficiency
apparent
incompetence

## UNIT 17

altar
alter
draught
draft
practice
practise
guest
guessed
morning
mourning
steel
steal
who's
whose
bruise
brews
heart
hart
accept
except
principle
principal
stationery
stationary
led
lead
ball
bawl

great
grate
wary
weary
device
devise
cereal
serial
ascent
assent
further
farther
bridal
bridle
prophet
profit
affect
effect
herd
heard
desert
dessert
compliments
complements
aisle
isle
proceed
precede
lightning
lightening
meddle
medal
license
licence
past
passed
aloud
allowed
descent
dissent
prophecy
prophesy
missed
mist
weather
whether
advice
advise
currant
current
patients
patience
wrung
rung

## UNIT 19

market
supermarket
committee
subcommittee
septic
antiseptic
categories
subcategories
stars
superstars
graph
autograph
conscious
subconscious
climax
anticlimax
marine
submarine
biographies
autobiographies

clockwise
anticlockwise
natural
supernatural
title
subtitle
human
superhuman
tract
subtract
theft
antitheft
anti-theft
man
superman
merged
submerged
mobiles
automobiles
glue
superglue
biotic
antibiotic
imposed
superimposed
divided
subdivided
way
subway
heading
subheading

computers
supercomputers
editor
subeditor

## UNIT 20

girl
girls
knave
knaves
tomato
tomatoes
celebration
celebrations
woman
women
mouse
mice
ibis
ibises
anniversary
anniversaries
foot
feet
man
men
sheep (singular)
sheep (plural)
privilege
privileges
rhythm
rhythms
ox
oxen
igloo
igloos
child
children
tooth
teeth
goose
geese
distillery
distilleries
attendee
attendees
fox
foxes
this
these
miniature
miniatures
wife

wives
cactus
cactuses
cacti
liability
liabilities
louse
lice
volcano
volcanoes
volcanos
allegory
allegories
loaf
loaves
crisis
crises
deer (singular)
deer (plural)
that
those
phenomenon
phenomena

children's
soldiers'
fishes
glasses
shoes'
controversies
scarves
amateurs'
firemen's
cookies
radios'
people's
cliffs
fungi
avocados
quizzes'
oases
puppies'
series
hippopotamuses

UNIT 21

begin
beginner
garden
gardener
communicate
communicator
forget

forgotten
limit
limitation
equip
equipped
sunburn
sunburnt
sunburned
ship
shipping
occur
occurring
nag
nagging
prepare
preparations
acquit
acquitted
engine
engineer
bargain
bargaining
overpopulate
overpopulation
babysit
babysitter
shoulder
shouldered
strum
strummed
carry
carrier

accommodated
insuring
formatted
emitting
unfocused
embarrassment
development
eavesdropper
pronounced
exaggerated

UNIT 22

conference
deferral
difference
suffered
offered
inferred
surfing
reference

referral
preference
differing
conferred
referendum
transference
pilfering
refereed

deference
conferring
deferred
offering
inference
pilfered
suffering
surfer
preferred
interfere

UNIT 23

music
musician
commit
commission
decide
decision
educate
education
discuss
discussion
adopt
adoption
include
inclusion
operate
operation
suggest
suggestion
electric
electrician
predict
prediction
express
expression
submit
submission
elect
election
promote
promotion
divide
division

comprehend
comprehension
attend
attention
compress
compression
insert
insertion
diffuse
diffusion
omit
omission
distort
distortion
suspend
suspension
profess
profession
graduate
graduation
project
projection
devote
devotion
contract
contraction
clinic
clinician
prevent
prevention
transmit
transmission

illustrate
illustration
optic
optician
impress
impression
pollute
pollution
admit
admission
confuse
confusion
confess
confession
indicate
indication
except
exception
permit
permission
exhaust

exhaustion
explode
explosion
statistic
statistician
intend
intention
accommodate
accommodation
digest
digestion
intrude
intrusion
desert
desertion
emit
emission

## UNIT 25

supervision
interested
disarm
inaudible
superb
antic
miscalculate
ill-advised
comet
expose
contract
profess
discos
preen
extraordinary
counter
unabridged
relative
reapplied
misfire
increase
inner
ungrammatical
prologue
mister
rebuilt
comma
discolour
coining
exclude
pronoun
extraterrestrial
proudly
reedy

intervene
imagine
autonomous
extract
dishonour
prowler
unrepentant
antique
indistinct
unit
misplaced
comely
convert
redeliver
condor
disown
unresolvable
inequality
under
profiterole
proactive
interred
disqualify
refill
exclaim
prodigy
subcontinent
mistletoe
misremembered
external
interim
inhibit
supersede
intern
properly
dissatisfied
conical
insignificance
misdial
probing
extracurricular
extra-curricular

perceptible
imperceptible
professional
unprofessional
accessible
inaccessible
advantage
disadvantage
compromising
uncompromising
considerate

inconsiderate
characteristic
uncharacteristic
replaceable
irreplaceable
belief
disbelief
bearable
unbearable
insured
uninsured
animate
inanimate
eligible
ineligible
reconcilable
irreconcilable
regarded
disregarded
patriotic
unpatriotic
appropriate
inappropriate
remarkable
unremarkable
effective
ineffective

## UNIT 26

uninterested
discontinued
disturbance
unacknowledged
improper
improbably
irredeemable
interlaced
unfashionable
irrelevance
imprisonment
reallocated
subdivision
misdiagnose
disapprovingly
undrinkable
re-evaluation
inadmissible
redoubling
unadvertised
subscript
uninvited
automatic
impersonated

disoriented

irreparable
indefinable
undefinable
inexperience
encouragement
proficiency
irreverent
misgovernment
disagreement
inconsistent
inconsistency
disrespectful
reassurance
imprudence
unemployment
irretrievable

jab
jabbed
president
presidential
induce
inducible
guide
guidance
differ
differed
irritate
irritation
urge
urgency
obsess
obsession
chisel
chiselling
comply
compliant
invent
invention
hysteric
hysterical
hysterically
persuade
persuasion
rhetoric
rhetorician
able
ably
plod
plodder
transfer
transferring

erode
erosion
eerie
eerily
trek
trekked
classify
classifiable
idealistic
idealistically
conscience
conscientious
transgress
transgression
absorb
absorbent
forensic
forensically
consequent
consequential
occupy
occupancy
cohere
coherence
flog
flogging
complete
completion
success
succession

UNIT 27

mine
ours
boss
bosses
thief
thieves
chief
chiefs
complex
complexes
echo
echoes
bookworm
bookworms
his
theirs
anchovy
anchovies
alley
alleys
mattress

mattresses
puff
puffs
rhinoceros (singular)
rhinoceros (plural)
rhinoceroses
myself
ourselves
handkerchief
handkerchiefs
advice (singular)
advice (plural)
giraffe
giraffes
moose (singular)
moose (plural)
barracks (singular)
barracks (plural)
lampshade
lampshades
matchstick
matchsticks
commando
commandos
commandoes
index
indices
belief
beliefs
ally
allies
torpedo
torpedoes
yours (singular)
yours (plural)
confectionery
confectioneries
offspring (singular)
offspring (plural)
axe
axes
zero (singular noun)
zeros (plural noun)
archipelago
archipelagos
archipelagoes

animals
snakes
bison (plural)
lions
tigers
llamas
pictures

information
planets
ships
cargoes
cargos
luxuries
docks
roofs
cottages
tiles
years
spines
bookshelves
house's
oboes'
crescendos
hairs
chef's
carrots
potatoes
radishes
leeks
rhythms
tangos
calypsos
waltzes
flames
dragons'
nostrils
mouths
mosquitoes'
mosquitos'
mosquito
bites
shoes
yours
clothes
chairs
gnomes
hoaxes
fairies'
children

UNIT 28

drake
duck
rooster
hen
gander
goose
boar
sow
ram

ewe
tom
tigress
drone
stag
vixen
peahen
bull
cow

duke
duchess
bridegroom
groom
bride
heir
heiress
lord
lady
shepherd
shepherdess
son
daughter
waiter
waitress
brother
sister
abbot
abbess
manservant
maidservant
hero
heroine
steward
stewardess
Mr
Mrs
lad
lass
prince
princess
master
mistress
earl
countess
headmaster
headmistress
god
goddess
emperor
empress
sir
madam
actor

actress
sire
dam
sultan
sultana
wizard
warlock
witch
widower
widow
monk
nun
bachelor
spinster
uncle
aunt
marquis
marchioness
fiancé
fiancée
billy goat
nanny goat

## UNIT 29

pact
packed
eminent
imminent
were
we're
alms
arms
bazaar
bizarre
metal
mettle
aural
oral
foreword
forward
quartz
quarts
born
borne
reek
wreak
swot
swat
course
coarse
troop
troupe
steak

stake
duel
dual
sort
sought
naval
navel
cast
caste
wear
where
gorilla
guerrilla
suite
sweet
told
tolled
hale
hail
whine
wine
mowed
mode
lava
larva
guilt
gilt
they're
their
lone
loan
council
counsel
borders
boarders
hoard
horde
lessen
lesson
ads
adds
fêtes
Fates
laps
lapse
hangars
hangers
peel
peal
whet
wet
storey
story

Printed in Great Britain
by Amazon

80714594R00059